7 STEPS TO LIVING A GRACE FILLED LIFE

Take the steps with God Now!

Dr. Jonathan Kim

Copyright © 2024 Jonathan Dj Kim

All rights reserved.

ISBN: 979-8-9897174-0-8

DEDICATION

To my sweet honey: Nancy Kim

Without her support and word of encouragement, this would never have happened

CONTENTS

	Acknowledgments	i
	Preface	1
	Introduction	3
	PART I: UNDERSTANDING OF WHO GOD IS	
1	STEP 1, KNOWING GOD	6
2	STEP 2, KNOWING CHRIST	21
3	STEP 3, KNOWING THE HOLY SPIRIT	33
	PART II: LIVING A BALANCED LIFE KNOWING WHO GOD IS AND WHO WE ARE	
4	STEP 4, KNOWING OTHERS	44
5	STEP 5, LIVING AS A GOD'S CHILD	61
6	STEP 6, LIVING AS A GOOD STEWARD	81
7	STEP 7, LIVING AS A DISCIPLE/WITNESS	97
	Conclusion	124
	Notes	126

ACKNOWLEDGMENTS

I want to express my deepest thanks to the following people:

To Johanna Kim, who took the time to review and offer her honest, critical critique of this book

To all who participate, for taking time out of their busy lives to contribute, directly and indirectly, to finishing the book with valuable insights.

PREFACE

In the modern church, there are many diverse people gathered together to seek faith and follow Christ; in the midst, there are those who know God, do not know God, want to know God, have the desire to grow in their faith, and those who want to serve and belong to a community of believers. The primary purpose is to educate the foundations of what it means to be a believer in Christ to all who belong to this community; thus, this book provides a simple, concise seven-step guide to a balanced life right now and in your future in Christ. These steps are so critical that no one can ignore them when developing a close relationship with God. Many questions, such as the following, pertain to understanding God and His plan and must be answered personally for one to truly live in God's presence: Who is God? What is His plan for His creation? What's God's providence? Who is Christ, and why did he come and die on the cross? What is God's sovereignty and fullness of God's grace? Who is Jesus? Is He truly a savior? Who is the Holy Spirit? What is His role? Why are there so many other religions or cults within Christianity? Who are we to God? What is our purpose? When is Jesus coming back? Are we all called to be disciples, stewards of what? What is going on right now? What are we waiting for? What does it mean to follow Jesus and live a balanced life? Each step one takes to know God, Christ, Holy Spirit, others, and ourselves as God's Children, stewards, and God's disciples will lead to and be able to deal with serious questions of believing in God through the reading; thus, one can fully comprehend God through the word and be able to live in the fullness of God's word.

INTRODUCTION

This book can not accomplish what God will do in one's life, but instead, it will bring and provide new insight into what it means to follow Jesus Christ and have faith in him. Many attend church without understanding their faith and live without a genuine relationship with God or one another. Eventually, amid trials, they fall out of church or live unfulfilled religious lives instead of living fulfilled, faithful lives God planned for them. This book will equip all to understand God and His plan, letting them take each necessary step to strengthen their faith and avoid falling into the sinking sand of unbelief. Thus, all those who seek faith will find an answer through the revelation of the truth in God's word. In return, they will understand who they are, why they are here, and where they are heading.

    Jesus Christ has commissioned all to be a witness[1] to others to proclaim the good news of him continually till His return.

---

[1] Matthew 29:30

What does it mean to be a faithful witness to this world? It means one must know God, Christ the Savior, and the work that the Holy Spirit is doing. Through knowing who God is, one will live a balanced life as a Child of God, a Good Steward, and a faithful witness, and stay on course to fulfill the commission Christ has instructed all to follow. Pray that God uses this book to give you all the proper steps to grow and live a balanced life as a faithful follower of Jesus Christ.

How to Use This Book

This book is intended to be read cover to cover, but, at the same time, it is to answer serious questions that could be done as a Bible study in a group. For this reason, the highlighted sections and scripture verses will be able to answer the questions directly and can be used as leverage to engage in conversation to further the depth of the studies, as to stay open for the constructive outcome from consensus within the group dynamic. This will eventually lead to one gaining further understanding and the ability to teach one another going forward. Thus, understanding and knowing God's word will bring forth structure and guidelines to become mature believers who will disciple and witness to others and the world.

PART ONE:

UNDERSTANDING OF WHO GOD IS

CHAPTER 1

STEP 1, KNOWING GOD

Who is God?

When one starts believing in God's existence, they will center their views on God. But, if there is doubt about God's existence, they will be centered on their thinking. For thousands of years, since its beginnings, thinkers have questioned God's existence. There are no differences in the past or now in searching for personal answers, the quest to find the answer to the question of origin and purpose to find identity in our world. If the truth remains unanswered, one's existence and purpose can lead to meaninglessness, which is why we all need an answer to the existence of God and who He is to all of us.[2] We will first find out whether God truly exists or not, we can't prove God's existence, but we will look at the evidence, looking at it from scripture rather than science; this book does not negate the importance of science and reason, just setting priority

---

[2] Romans 1:18-23

and focus on this book. Let's start with Psalms 14:1, "The fool has said in his heart, there is no God."[3] Immanuel Kant, a famous German philosopher, came to a foolish conclusion based on his understanding of truth and revelation, which tries to find an alternative to God; Kant proposes and enables the people to believe that they could genuinely live morally and well without God as alternative whereas a good society as the answer. Atheists foolishly believe and conclude that using science and evolution can provide an answer to everything. They mock creation or intelligent design as believing in fairy tales rather than being worthy of scientific or naturalistic examination, for science itself is the finding of what already exists.

To find the truth, one needs to know that the truth comes from the scripture; God created everything.[4] Even in my journey, God revealed himself to me through His word and revelation of His love in my years of searching. It plays a crucial role when coming into faith, but it's also essential to see what God personally reveals to one to find Him. There can be only acceptance when one commits their faith in the authority of Scripture, His attributes, His power, and nature. One will see the evidence of His love and how He seeks a relationship with Him.

God is a creator.

When God created the world and universe[5], out of nothing with His word, one could already see how powerful and majestic God is and how He is sustaining all His creation in balance by His declaration of His word, glory proclaimed through His handiwork.[6]

---

[3] New King James Version

[4] Genesis 1:1

[5] Genesis 1:1

[6] Psalm 19:1

For example, everything is created and aligned perfectly in the universe and solar systems, making Earth a unique place where we could dwell in. He is omnipotent (all-powerful), omniscient (all-knowing), and Omnipresent (all-present). But, what makes God who He is, as stated in Psalm 33:6, "By the word of the Lord the heavens were made, and all the host of them by the breath of His mouth." [7] When one speaks that God is omnipotent, He is sovereign, infinite, and powerful. Even Job acknowledges Him in his time of trials, where God is all-powerful and establishes His plan. In Job 42:2, "I know that you can do everything, And that no purpose of yours can be withheld from you." [8] One cannot truly comprehend His good plan at face value, with God's power and holiness it allows things to happen that one cannot fully understand. Thus, one requires faith in Him that possesses power where He created everything to fulfill His good plan out of nothing. [9]

    When He created the heavens and earth, He spoke[10] into them. But, He created mankind personally by forming a man from the dust and breathing into the nostril, thus becoming a living being.[11] The woman He created out of a man by taking a rib from his side. [12] He demonstrated how He created mankind with unique, special, and personal attention to show His intention of seeking something more out of his creation, that He is not just a creator, but one filled with Grace seeking relationship with the creation.

---

[7] New King James Version

[8] New King James Version

[9] Colossians 1:16

[10] Genesis 1:11-16

[11] Genesis 2:7

[12] Genesis 2:21

God as heavenly father

When one calls someone their father, there is respect; no one can deny the trust and uniqueness that exists in this relationship between father and son. Relationships grow deeper as one spends more time with one another, from strangers to developing a more personal relationship that carries importance. In today's society, fatherhood has been so distorted by the media and culture that the respect that once existed for the term father has been lost. Thus, it is hard to understand God as a father truly. God is our Father because He has created everything to seek a relationship with us.[13] But Satan not only distorted the relationship God created for good; He also destroyed the relationship.[14] Still, God loved us when He sent His beloved son to die on the cross, restoring the lost relationship and now mended completely through His redemption plan through Christ.[15] God imputed our sin to the account of Jesus Christ.

We must consider who we were without Christ and who we become with Christ. We were born in sin[16] and were guilty of breaking God's holy laws.[17] We were enemies of God[18], deserving of death.[19] We were unrighteous,[20] and without means of justifying

---

[13] Genesis 1:1

[14] Genesis 3:1-5

[15] Genesis 3:15, Genesis 3:21, Romans 8:17

[16] Psalm 51:5

[17] Romans 3:9–20, 23 ,1 John 1:8–10

[18] Romans 5:6, 10, 8.7 ,Colossians 1:21

[19] Romans 6:23

[20] Romans 3:10

ourselves.[21] Spiritually, we were destitute, blind, unclean, and dead. Our souls were in peril of everlasting punishment, but with God's plan through Jesus Christ, we are filled with hope now and forever.

What is His plan? God's plan through creation

God's plan started with His creation, and He made clear His purpose behind His creation when He created Adam and Eve. He seeks to have a relationship with His creation, more to do with mankind; why? It is for His pleasure. What, one may ask? Isn't it selfish? One must understand that God is the creator, and when He creates, there is pleasure in His creation. When one makes something extraordinary, when completed, there can be only joy in seeing the creation. Genesis 1:27, is written, made in the image and likeness of God[22], thus, the ability to understand firsthand what it means to love and have fellowship with God. Some may believe that He is lonely because He seeks a relationship with His creation. This is far from the truth; the perfect relationship exists through the tribune nature of God, and as God mentioned I'm that I am.[23] But, one may ask God why He would destroy His creation with a flood. God is not silent on His reason for the destruction of His creation. In Genesis 6:5-6, "Then the Lord saw that the wickedness of man was great in the earth and that every intent of the thoughts of His heart was only evil continually. And the Lord was sorry that He had made man on the earth, and He was grieved in His heart." [24] Even today, it is true that all those living sins and disobeying God's call to turn to Him with repented hearts and continuously rejecting God's gift through Jesus Christ caused the Holy Spirit to

---

[21] Romans 3:20

[22] New King James Version

[23] Exodus 3:14

[24] Genesis 6:7-9

grieve. But, still, God is patient until the final second for them to turn to Him, but this is a reminder that there will be times for judgment when His righteous judgment has to be delivered so that the righteousness will prevail and be with Him forever.

Noah's story

When one recalls Noah's flood, one may ask how a loving God would bring such destruction to His creation. At the time of Noah, there was corruption and perversion. God grieved the actions of mankind for their wickedness. But, Noah found favor in the eyes of the Lord[25], and He walked with God[26], although He was not perfect, He was righteous, blameless, and obedient to God. God responds with judgment upon wicked people in His holy way, where God cannot allow wickedness to continue. He cannot allow injustice and ungodliness to continue that goes against His nature. Thus, God perished those who committed wickedness and saved the righteous ones. He will bring His righteous judgment to this world in His perfect time, where He is waiting on more people to turn to His love.

His plan through Israelites

One could always ask why God chose Israel as His chosen nation where Christ will be born. When Adam and Eve fell into temptation, His redemption plan started, and God promised Abraham that the Messiah, Jesus Christ, would come from His descendants. He chose the Israelites to reveal Himself and show the world that Israelites, as distant nations, set apart for Him, also to bring the Messiah, Jesus Christ, who will save the world. He picks Abraham, Moses, and David to show that He is God who

---

[25] New King James Version

[26] New King James Version

delivers promises and keeps His word.

Choosing Abram

God calls Abraham out of nowhere. Abraham's father was a tradesman who sold idols at Ur of Chaldees. Abraham did not know God nor did he know he would be called the nation's father. God chose Him to be the first Hebrew patriarch and prophet[27], and the nation that will bring forth Messiah, Jesus Christ.[28] Abraham's confidence in God grew from a single step of faith as God's character and purpose were revealed to Him. Abraham's faith went beyond a statement of trust in God's provision. Faith finds expressions in words; it results in action, often sacrifice, demonstrated by Abram, such as when he demonstrated the willingness to trust God and offer his son on the altar. God demonstrated His mighty power and personal involvement with Abram throughout his journey.

Moses

Moses was chosen by God and God's protection was demonstrated throughout his life. Especially when Israelite babies were to be killed and when he faced death, he was saved by Pharaoh's daughter and an act of courage from Miriam. Also, Moses was raised with the mind of one-day ruling as Pharaoh. But God had a different plan in mind for Moses, as his heart yearned for his people and stood up for his people. He was eager to save his people from mistreatment, so he rushed and committed murder to defend the Israelites. Why would God use Moses to save his people? He uses his imperfections of earlier years, where he killed

---

[27] Romans 3:2

[28] Galatians 3:16

the Egyptian[29], to reveal a great plan of redemption by calling at old age to lead his people out of Egypt. God uses those willing to follow Him and His way. For the later part of his life, Moses put his trust in Him and followed God and His word. Moses saved his people from darkness, bondage, and slavery, but through the grace of God, he was used to deliver his people to the Promised Land. Jesus died on the cross to save humanity from the darkness of sin and bring hope through Him.

David

A little shepherd boy, came ready to fight Goliath, a giant Philistine warrior mocking God, to teach him a lesson and the Philistines of the power of God. Can one imagine the scene? David came forward with judgment towards Goliath for speaking against God. God prepared him for the battle by equipping him with the tools he used to steer away wild animals while shepherding. Also, God gave David victory for standing up against those who mock God. Eventually, David became king of Israel and set up the nation of Israel. Why did God choose David? God chose him by looking at David's heart.[30] The true King, Jesus Christ, Messiah, comes from David's line. David seeks, after God's own heart.[31] Jesus Christ would lay His life for humanity to demonstrate His love.

His plan through Christ

Jesus Christ fulfills God's plan completely. God's plan for Christ is to make people see Him through Christ and His love. God revealed himself in the Old Testament since the creation to be with Israelites, as one provides law and guidance. Before Jesus, like in

---

[29] Exodus 2:14

[30] 1 Samuel 16:7

[31] 1 Samuel 13:13-14

old Levitical sacrifices were not completed, they did not take away sin completely; they needed one who could take away sin completely through the perfect sacrifice.

God's providence on sin, the sovereignty of His will, and grace

When one looks at God's plan, through beginning and end, one can only ask the questions of sin, His grace, and sovereignty over His plan. Why would He allow this to happen? God created men with free will; without choice, men will be robots, with the potential risk of making a choice that goes against His word and sub consequences. Free will means one's ability to choose one's will. God did not create sin or delight in those who rebel and commit sin, but His desire and plan for all to come to receive His love and experience the joy of His presence and everlasting life that is with Him.

The problem of God's sovereignty comes into light when one deals with the issue of free will. How would this be possible? God is all-powerful and all-knowing[32] and responsible for His creation.[33] One questions all man's choices, and it ultimately falls under God's sovereignty. One needs to recognize that God has the power to do anything, but God often chooses not to act directly and allows it. Thus, everything that happens, at least, happens due to God's permissive will, even if certain things are not what He wants. Allowing the permissive will truly demonstrate the sovereignty over all things, as to act or not, whenever and whatever.

God's purpose, His will, always focuses on humanity, as

---

[32] Psalm 147:5

[33] Genesis 1:1

His creation, to be in His presence and love. Meanwhile, with the rejection of His love and the temptation of Satan, God had to allow the consequences of their sins to manifest. Still, with His grace[34] and love[35], He chose to redeem mankind by making a way to be renewed and have a relationship with Him. He showed His grace that one does not deserve.

His righteous judgment in the Old Testament

At the same time, He showed that He stands for righteousness and holiness. He judges according to His righteousness. God showed His mercy toward the judgment of Adam and Eve by sacrificing animals to clothe them, but Adam and Eve had to bear the consequences of their action, which was to face death and be forbidden from the Garden of Eden.

The judgment came down for the wickedness[36] of Noah's time, where the flood destroyed all mankind and animals except for Noah and his family. The evil heart and wickedness of the people made God grieve and foresee the outcome. But, He saw through Noah and his righteousness[37], and that He was faithful in waiting on the Lord as he continually built the ark, even amassing pressure and mockery from wicked people. Thus, they were saved from the judgment of God.

God delivers His righteous judgment at the Tower of Babel.[38] People were filled with pride and came together to be like God, and they disobeyed God by building the tower that would

---

[34] Ephesians 2:8

[35] John 3:16

[36] Genesis 6:5

[37] Genesis 6:7-8

[38] Genesis 11:1-9

reach heaven. Thus, God disperses them by confusing their language. They left according to language and settled in different regions of the world.[39]

Abraham's nephew, Lot, chose to live in a city consumed with sin.[40] Because of the sinful lifestyle many were committing, God decided to bring forth the destruction of the neighboring cities with fiery sulfur. As a result, the city of Sodom and Gomorrah was destroyed. Yet, God showed mercy upon Lot and his family because Abraham interceded and asked for God's mercy for the sake of righteous people, but there were not. Thus, God sends an angel to save Lot's family from punishment.

The judgment of Egypt and their gods, as Egyptians punished Israelites unfairly for 400 years, God brought upon the ten plagues to change Pharaoh's heart to free the Israelites from the bondage of slavery.

Korah was the leader of a rebellion known as Korah's Rebellion. He is the son of Kohath from the tribe of Levi, which is from the same tribe as Moses and Aaron. Korah believed he could lead the Israelites better than Moses and challenged Moses' leadership.[41] But he was unaware that he was going against God. God was with Moses, and Moses tested the authority which Korah spoke of, whether from God or not. As a result, God opened up and swallowed them.[42] God was not done with the Israelites as they complained about Moses and Aaron, who brought forward the killing of God's people. But, Moses and Aaron prayed and interceded so that God would stop His righteous wrath and kill

---

[39] Genesis 11:8-9

[40] Genesis 18:20

[41] Numbers 16:3

[42] Numbers 16:31-35

more Israelites[43]. Like Korah's rebellion, Israelites continually witnessed God's righteous wrath upon Israelites and enemies of God.

His righteous judgment in the New Testament

Jesus took the judgment of sin and suffered death to demonstrate the grace of God. Thus, God called each one's heart to self-exam with prayer, the condition of their faith in God by purifying through the work of Christ on the cross. Each believer will be led by the Holy Spirit and have the same mind, becoming like Christ by following Jesus's example. God allows hardships to the believer, thus, developing more endurance as one puts their faith in His deliverance.[44]

His righteous judgment in the second coming

Christ foretells when He will come back at His ascension[45], He will return as the judging King who will bring forth God's judgment. The Book of Revelation details a sign describing God's judgment against the wicked: seven seals, seven trumpets, and seven bowls.[46] Ultimately, it all points to the nation of Israel coming before God with repentance. For those who accepted Christ, God will reward those who have kept their faith in giving glory through their heart toward God; this is not referencing anything to do with sin that Christ paid; it pertains only to serving faithfully in building God's kingdom. Crowns[47] will be given as a reward for being righteous and living in faith to share the love of God. The world will face

---

[43] Numbers 16:41-50

[44] Hebrews 12:5-11

[45] Acts 1:9-11

[46] Revelation 6-16

[47] Revelation 3:11

judgment after the tribulation based on how they treated Israel, His nation. Also, fallen angels will face the judgment of God[48] and the final judgment of the great white throne; unbelievers are judged and thrown into the lake of fire. God's judgment which everyone has to face, will be in a form that is different based on their faith or faithlessness. God is compassionate, gracious, slow to anger, faithful, and abound in love. God wants the sinner to turn to Christ, the savior who brings saving grace from God, to turn away from judgment and receive God's mercy. Only hope can come through the resurrection and promise of our Lord Jesus Christ's return., as one turns away from the things of this world and keep God's word. [49]

---

[48] Jude 1:6

[49] 1 John 3:1, 1 John 2:5, 1 John 2:15

Group Discussion

Leaders: Explain why it is important to know who God is by asking questions about what they know about God. You could answer first or ask the members to start first. Go through the questions and answer by finding the reference bible verses.

1. Who is God to you?

2. Why do people have such a hard time believing in God? Psalm 14:1

3. What does the Bible say about not believing? Romans 1:18-23

4. How did God create the world, and with what? Genesis 1:1, Psalm 33:6, Colossians 1:16

5. Is God's plan better than our plan? Job 42:2

6. How is it different for His creation over man? Genesis 2:7, Genesis 2:21

7. How does God make us? Genesis 1:27

8. What is God's name? Exodus 3:14

9. Why were Noah and His family saved by God from judgment? Genesis 6:7-8

10. What was the reason behind choosing Israelites? John 3:16

11. Why did God Choose Abraham, who did not know Him? Genesis 22:1-18, Galatians 3:16

12. Why would God use Moses to save His people?

13. Did Moses kill Egyptians, and for what reason? Exodus 2:14

14. Why did God choose David? 1 Samuel 16:7

15. What does God's sovereignty show us about who He is? Ephesians 2:8-9

16. Is God truly all-powerful and all-knowing? Psalm 147:5

17. Why did God have to judge the world through the flood? Genesis 6:5

18. Why did God decide to confuse the language of the people? Genesis 11:1-9

19. How will Christ return in the second coming? Acts 1:9-11

20. What does it mean when you are in love with the world? 1 John 2:15

CHAPTER 2

STEP 2, KNOWING CHRIST

Who is Jesus?

The answer to this question will vary significantly based on who you ask. But Jesus said that He and God the Father are one[50], equal to God. He existed in creation[51]; He was a real person in history; He was of virgin birth, ministered for three years, persecuted and died on the cross, and was resurrected, and many witnessed Jesus ascending into heaven with the promise of returning. Jesus offered salvation to those who come in faith and, through believing in Him, will receive truth and life.[52]

Jesus as Rabbi or Teacher

---

[50] John 10:30

[51] John 8:58

[52] John 14:6

First, one needs to know what a Jewish Rabbi or Teacher means in Jewish traditions, which is the synonymous title; it means a member of the clergy in Judaism. The role involves teaching and instruction in Jewish traditions, interpreting, and being considered wise. John the Baptist also was called to be Rabbi.[53] Jesus was referred to as a Rabbi by others even though He was not part of the temple because He often taught and interpreted God's word. Nicodemus thought it was fitting for Jesus to be called Rabbi in John 3:2: "Rabbi, we know that You are a teacher come from God; for no one can do these signs that You do unless God is with him." [54]

Jesus as Messiah

Jesus of Nazareth was called Messiah or Anointed among the people following Him during His ministry. Of course, there were also those calling Him a liar and persecuting Him. Before Christ, the prophecy regarding the coming of the Messiah was known through the Old Testament, and Jews were waiting for the Messiah. The Old Testament prophecies are about Messiah's birth, who He is, what He will be doing, and how he will die are all fulfilled by Christ. He fulfilled the prophecy of the virgin birth, a virgin will be with a child[55], and in Isaiah 9:6,"a child who will be the prince of peace will be born."[56] In Micah 5:2, "one who will be ruler over Israel"[57], and in Psalm 22:16-18 speaks of "how evil men will divide

---

[53] John 3:26

[54] New King James Version

[55] John 1:1,14

[56] New King James Version

[57] New King James Version

up the garment"[58], be pierced[59], and face death and thus bring forth righteousness and salvation.[60] There is no doubt that this is, Jesus Christ, our Lord Savior. Jesus Christ fulfilled all prophecies, a prophet[61], a priest[62], and a king.[63]

Jesus as the Son of God

Jesus is God, manifested in human form, conceived by the Holy Spirit[64], where God Himself enters the world as a man. Of course, Jesus did not directly say He is God but claimed to be God by replying to Jews that the Father and I are equal, and there can not be any doubt of His response of who He is to them.[65] Jesus came to pay the penalty for the sins of the world[66], which only God himself could be able to do.[67] Some question the deity of Christ, John 3:16, "only begotten", monogenesis, could be misinterpreted to mean that Jesus Christ is a created being, rather than the 2nd person of the Trinity. He is the one and only Son of God, clearly mentioned in John 20:31 of His nature as God[68], different from us

---

[58] New King James Version

[59] Zechariah 12:10

[60] Zechariah 9:9

[61] Deuteronomy 18:18

[62] Psalm 110:4

[63] Isaiah 11:1-14

[64] Isaiah 11:1-14

[65] John 10:30-33

[66] 1 John 2:2

[67] Romans 5:8

[68] New King James Version

adopted as God's child.[69]

Why did Jesus come? To proclaim God's plan.

Jesus came to fulfill God's plan to save humanity, as predicted throughout the Old Testament, God's redemptive plan. He showed to all that He came with a purpose and acted according to God's plan, His father's.[70] He knew what to do. In His ministry, He came for the poor and those forgotten by the so-called righteous leaders such as Pharisees, Sadducees, and chief priests. His ministry encircles healing and forgiving the sinners for turning their life to God through accepting His invitation of hope that exists through Him. He came to save the sinners.[71] He came to those who are lost, perfectly reflected in the story of the prodigal son.[72] He wants those who come to Him to receive peace and repent.[73] He teaches that God wants more than following the law, obeying His word, and believing in Christ for salvation through Him and the coming days of judgment.

To reveal God the Father

Israelites experienced God firsthand, who was with them throughout their wilderness journey. He is the creator, lawgiver, redeemer, and judge, displaying His eternal power and divine nature (Romans 1:20).[74] Jesus represents God the Father perfectly

---

[69] Ephesians 1:5

[70] Luke 2:49

[71] Matthew 9:13

[72] Luke 15:1-10

[73] Luke 15:21-22

[74] Romans 1:20

(Hebrews 1:3).[75] In John 1:18, "No one has ever seen God."[76] When one sees Jesus, you have seen the Father responding to Philip[77] and teaching him to know the truth through his experienced with Him. Jesus reveals God's love through His sacrifice on the cross by facing death.[78] Also, throughout His ministry, he showed how one would fully understand God's love and His plan through His teaching, healing, and sacrifices.

To deal with sin and save the lost

God bestowed laws to deal with sins by offering sacrifice on the altar in the Old Testament, where the continuous offering was needed for cleansing.[79] But, through Jesus Christ, offering himself as a final sacrifice for all, there is no need of continuous offering as required in the Old Testament. God forgave people who were lost due to their sins by letting Christ die on the cross and releasing them from the bondage of sin; thus, His people will stay away from sin. God is the only true Savior.[80] Through Christ, there can be only hope and salvation that God gave those lost. For Christ justified[81], have peace through Him and the promise of eternal life, spending forever in the presence of God, sealed by the Spirit[82] at the moment of faith. In Romans 8:30, mentions justification and

---

[75] Hebrews 1:3

[76] New King James Version

[77] John 14:9

[78] Romans 5:8

[79] Hebrew 9:26

[80] Hosea 13:4

[81] Romans 5:1

[82] Ephesians 1:13-14

glorification by Christ, where salvation is the gift of God.[83]

To judge the world

Jesus came as a savior[84] and a suffering servant who offered God's love through His sacrifice on the cross. But, He will return as a King who will judge, where the authority to judge is given by God.[85] In Acts 1:11, He will return the same way He ascended.[86] The Location is also prophesied and known in Zechariah 14:4, Mount of Olives[87], and also signs and wonders will show.[88] When it happens, it will be the glorious moment that demonstrates God's power and majesty in full display.[89] There will be a judgment on those who reject Him[90] and fallen angels.[91] Since Jesus is God and Man, He will be a perfect judge to preside over the believer and unbeliever; fair and righteous judgment will be delivered to all.

What does it mean to have a personal relationship with Him?

To accept Him as the Son of God

Jesus is the Son of God. Some may find this hard to believe and have difficulty accepting the truth. This tends to occur when we base it on our own experience, but when we base it on the scripture

---

[83] New King James Version

[84] John 3:16

[85] John 5:22-23

[86] New King James Version

[87] New King James Version

[88] Matthew 24:30

[89] Titus 2:13

[90] John 9:39

[91] John 12:31-33

and through His words; we will see that Jesus truly is the Son of God. For that reason, we need to know the Scripture and what the Scripture said about Himself. Mary witnessed the visit from an angel who let her know that the Holy Spirit would impregnate her and be called the Son of God[92] and comforted her; there is no misunderstanding of who Christ is, even before His birth, confirmed by the Holy Spirit and witnessed by Mary. When Christ was asked by the High Priest[93] whether He was the Son of God, He responded according to what He had asked. He is the one who is sitting at the right of God.[94] For being the son of God, His death on the cross is sufficient to pay the penalty for the sins; created beings cannot pay the penalty of sin against God. Only the Son of God could bear the sins of the world by being obedient to God's calling to die to save the lost, to declare victory over death and sin. Now, knowing this truth through the scripture, one can accept and acknowledge that He is the son of God, who died on the cross to save the world.

To accept Him as Messiah, one fulfilled the Old Testament prophecy.

Accepting Jesus as Messiah pertains more to Jews, but even to us, it carries significance. It validates who He is through the Old Testament Prophecy and how the fulfillment of prophecy reassures us all to trust in who He is. The Book Matthew focuses on Jesus coming as Messiah. Matthew connected the Old and New by referencing Messiah. [95] There is no doubt that Jesus came as a

---

[92] Luke 1:35

[93] Matthew 26:63

[94] Matthew 26:64

[95] Matthew 1:16

suffering servant[96] and faced suffering along with death on the cross, and was buried in the tomb[97] and resurrected. To accept Christ as Messiah confirms that one believes in Jesus as Lord and Savior; to deny means the spiritual blindness of one who has been clouded by the ambition of this world and distortion of the deception of Satan.

To accept Him personally as Savior by faith

If one attends a church, this does not automatically make them a believer. A true reflection of being a genuine Christian is someone who has accepted Jesus Christ, and their lives are transformed to be like Christ and live as a new creation through Christ. To accept Christ, one needs to know that God gave us a gift of eternal salvation through Jesus Christ, just as God granted righteousness to Abraham as a gift. Most think Abraham did something to earn God's grace through faith by offering Isaac, his son, when God asked Abraham to sacrifice Isaac on the altar. But Abraham received God's gift of grace through his son living because God had already provided a sacrificial lamb instead of Isaac; Jesus Christ became one who was sacrificed. The famous verse from Habakkuk 2:4, "Just shall live by his faith," [98] is fulfilled in the righteousness that comes by faith in the gospel of Christ. His death on the cross and resurrection fulfilled God's plan to save us. Our imperfect faith does not justify us but by the perfect righteousness of Christ. The natural man such as us cannot indeed reach out to accept the salvation of God in Christ. We are dead in trespasses and sin. The sinner does not move toward God, but God first moves towards a sinner to unite him with Christ by faith. The hand of faith graciously and unconditionally receives and rests upon Christ and

---

[96] Isaiah 53

[97] Mark 15:27

[98] New King James Version

His righteousness alone. Thus, faith is nothing less than the means which unites a sinner with his savior. By acknowledging through faith that the grace of God saves us, Christ came and died for our sins[99] and paid the price on the cross for our sins, resulting in accepting the gift of God. Thus, we need to accept the gift from God and give glory to God throughout our lives.

To live through following His teaching

Jesus taught those listening to Him that with mustard seed faith, we can expect new, more challenging opportunities for our faith to mature, even under very uncomfortable circumstances. Each opportunity to grow in faith tends to come as a statement about God followed by proper action. Jesus asks and invites you to step onto a solid rock of faith and experience the results. He does not point to things we can have or what He might do. He points to Himself.

Jesus' calls include practical applications to last a lifetime. We need to turn from sin, believing that God offers something better than sinful, earthly pleasures, and obeying His command to love others neither requires faith, even if others do not return our love. His purposes for our lives surpass our ambitions. The Deepening faith challenges common sense, which is hard to understand or do. We are inclined to assess the situation before we act. But Jesus continually reminds us that all the evidence is within us and takes the step of faith to accept. As faith deepens, we accept the truth and act on it. There is a difference between faith and presumption. Faith challenges typically start with God speaking; his voice is always consistent with Scripture. The presumption needs a record to point to. With a growing faith, we experience increased blessings and the extraordinary presence of God. Everyone who

---

[99] Romans 5:8

witnessed Christ in their life, despite their initial fears and low expectations, their faith grew, and they witnessed more of God's glory. When God challenges us, we must follow what Jesus taught us and apply it in our lives.

Group Discussion

Leaders: Explain why it is important to know who Jesus is to them and share your experience of coming to know Christ. Then, go through the questions and answer by finding the reference bible verses.

1. Did Jesus get involved in creation in Genesis? If He did, how did

it get involved? Genesis 1:16

2. What did Nicodemus call Jesus? Why? John 3:2

3. Did people consider John the Baptist as Rabbi? John 3:26

4. What are some Old Testament prophecies mentioned about Jesus as messiah? Isaiah 7:14, Isaiah 9:6 Micah 5:2, Psalm 22:16-18, Isaiah 53:3-7, Zechariah 12:10, Zechariah 9:9, Psalm 110:4, Isaiah 11:1-4

5. Why do some question the deity of Christ as a created being? John 3:16

6. What does scripture say about Jesus as the Son of God? John 20:31

7. Why did Jesus come, by whose plan? Luke 2:49

8. Why did He come for sinners, not for those who are righteous leaders? Matthew 9:13

9. What does Jesus want for the sinner, in comparison to the prodigal son, to do and receive? Luke 15:21-22

10. Can one see God through Jesus? John 14:9

11. Did God show His love through Jesus? Romans 5:8

12. Are we justified faith on our own or through Christ? Romans 5:1

13. How do we know that our faith is real? Ephesians 1:13-14

14. Who gave authority to Jesus Christ to judge the world? John 5:22-23

15. Where is the location of Jesus's second coming? Zechariah

14:4

16. What will happen in Jesus' second coming? Matthew 24:30

17. What will happen to those who reject Jesus and fallen angels? John 9:39, John 12:31-133

18. What did Mary hear from the angel about what will happen to her? Luke 1:35

19. Where is Jesus, the Son of God? Matthew 26:64

20. What did Jesus do for us? Romans 5:8

CHAPTER 3

STEP 3, KNOWING THE HOLY SPIRIT

Who is the Holy Spirit?

There has been so much misinterpretation and false understanding of who the Holy Spirit is and the work of the Holy Spirit. Many wonder who the Holy Spirit is; some say that it is the extension of God, a force. Thus, there needs to be clarification and understanding of who the Holy Spirit is to us.

God

The Holy Spirit is God, the third person of the Trinity, and has His will, mind, and emotions, who righteously deserves our love and for us to surrender to Him. The scripture confirms that the Holy Spirit is not an extension of the power of God but rather a separate divine being, such as when Peter confronts Ananias about lying to the Holy Spirit.[100] Ananias broke his promise by keeping a portion of the profit from the land that had been sold. As a result, he died for his lies to the Holy Spirit. Fear comes over him, and he dies out of breath. Just like God the Father, the Holy Spirit possesses a divine nature, omniscient[101], and omnipresent.[102] The Holy Spirit partakes in creation.[103] At Jesus' Baptism, the Spirit descends on him like a dove, and Father acknowledges from heaven that He is pleased with His beloved Son Jesus Christ. [104]

In the same way, no one knows the thoughts of God except the Spirit of God." The Holy Spirit thinks and knows. [105] The Holy Spirit can be grieved[106] as one rejects and speaks the lies by deceiving one another. The Spirit intercedes for us[107] when facing our weakness. He makes decisions according to His will[108] to profit for those who need wisdom. As God, the Holy Spirit can function as the Comforter and Counselor Jesus promised He would be.[109]

Helper, Comforter, and Guide

The Holy Spirit is a person and divine being, thus infinitely holy,

---

[100] Acts 5:3-4

[101] 1 Corinthians 2:10-11

[102] Psalm 139:7-8

[103] Genesis 1:2

[104] Mark 1:10-11

[105] 1 Corinthians 2:10

[106] Ephesians 4:30

[107] Romans 8:26-27

[108] 1 Corinthians 12:7-11

[109] John 14:16, 26; 15:26

wise, and tender, who is involved with us daily to get hold of us, to lead and use us for God's will. In John 14:26, "But the Helper, the Holy Spirit, whom the Father will send in My name, He will teach you all things, and bring to your remembrance all things that I said to you." [110] Jesus made a promise to His disciples as He departed, assuring them the Holy Spirit would be there and would not be alone when they continued the good works that He had commissioned for them to fulfill. The Holy Spirit will teach all things that will equip them. Also, the Holy Spirit will counsel those who seek encouragement and fill hope in the hearts of believers in times of uncertainty, trials, and persecution.[111] Jesus knew the disciples were downright because Christ was not there to comfort them through His presence; thus, He promised the helper, the Holy Spirit. The Holy Spirit acts as a guide, an intercessor, and thus, helps us in prayer. We do not know how or ought to pray, but He intercedes before God through His will.[112] He dwells in our hearts and knows us of everything we do, see, act, speak, and think. Thus, the Holy Spirit knows and leads one to move away from the unholy life and brings one into the presence of God. We cannot ignore the truth of how He is personal and speaks with depths of wisdom to those who are listening to hear the truth of God.

What is the role of the Holy Spirit? To fulfill God's plan.

The Spirit of God was present, hovering over the waters and involved in the creation;[113] also, through Him, the moon and stars were created.[114] When Job replies to his friend's foolish advice,

---

[110] New King James Version

[111] Romans 8:9, 1 Corinthians 6:19-20

[112] Romans 8:26-27

[113] Genesis 1:2

[114] Psalm 33:6

instead of rebuking, Job reminds him how majestic God is and emphasizes that the Spirit of God was the one who made heaven beautiful[115] The Holy Spirit moved the prophets of God with the words of God[116] "for prophecy never came by the will of man, but holy men of God spoke as they were moved by the Holy Spirit" and empowers God's people. [117]

In the conception of Jesus Christ, a similar "hovering" of the Holy Spirit is mentioned: "And the angel answered and said to Mary, 'The Holy Spirit will come upon you, and the power of the Highest will overshadow you'"[118] Also in creation, God breathes into the nostril of man[119] "spirit," enters and gives life. Also, the Holy Spirit gave life to man and other living creatures.[120]

In the Old Testament, the Holy Spirit was in works through God's servants. Joshua is about to become a leader of the Israelites; God commissions him and acknowledges the Holy Spirit within him to guide him to the Promised Land. [121] Gideon, a chosen leader to fight off the oppression of Midiantes Israelites, was led by the Spirit of God. [122]

Samson, from his conception, God gave his parents instructions on how the baby should be raised and led by the

---

[115] Job 26:13

[116] 2 Peter 1:21

[117] Zechariah 4:6

[118] Luke 1:35

[119] Genesis 2:7

[120] Psalm 104:29, 30

[121] Numbers 27:18

[122] Judges 6:34

Spirit[123], and strength was given by the Holy Spirit when he was faced with danger. In the case of Saul, God chose and blessed him to become the new king of the Israelites, but he started envying David for his growing stature. He disobeyed God, the Spirit of God; thus, the Holy Spirit eventually departed from Saul[124], and he was filled with a distressing Spirit. But, David was filled with the spirit of the Lord, continually speaking to him. [125] Ezekiel also experienced a similar experience, filled with the Spirit and spoke to him[126] as he was called to be a prophet to rebuke the Israelites for their disobedience. Jesus, the Messiah, will fulfill the prophecy in Isaiah 61:1-2. "The Spirit of the Lord God is upon Me Because the Lord has anointed Me to preach good tidings to the poor; He has sent Me to heal the brokenhearted, To proclaim liberty to the captives, And the opening of the prison to those who are bound;" [127] where the Holy Spirit inspired Isaiah to prophecy in Isaiah 11:2: "The Spirit of the Lord shall rest upon Him."[128]

God plans to equip the believers for their work to proclaim the good news of Jesus Christ. After the Holy Spirit came, the disciples were equipped for their work, and we see them powerfully proclaiming the gospel of Jesus Christ. [129] The Holy Spirit guided them into the truth[130] and brought to their

---

[123] Judges 13:25; 14:6

[124] 1 Samuel 10:9, 10, 14

[125] 2 Samuel 23:2

[126] Ezekiel 2:2

[127] New King James Version

[128] New King James Version

[129] Acts 2-4

[130] John 16:13

remembrance what Jesus had said.[131]

To help the believers

When one accepts Christ as personal savior, the Holy Spirit gives the believer belief in God and the salvation of eternal life. His very nature is pure and divine[132], and the Holy Spirit comes to live within Him spiritually. The fact that the believer's body is likened to a temple[133] where the Holy Spirit lives helps us to understand the indwelling of the Holy Spirit. When one thinks of the word temple, it may seem unfamiliar since we now have a church instead of a temple. But, in the Old Testament, the temple is closely related and described as the Holy of Holies in the Tabernacle. As Israelites were on the journey in the wilderness, through the instruction given by God, they built the Tabernacle. God met them in the Tabernacle, where the Holy of Holies is in the innermost sacred place where it's forbidden; only the high priest could come in once a year to perform the sacrifice and receive forgiveness from God. Thus, the believer's body is a holy temple and needs to know that the believers should live to give glory, for God is with the believer.

Jesus taught the disciples to go and share the good news and be baptized in the name of the Father, Son, and Holy Spirit, not just His name, but in tribune God, because the Holy Spirit will bring forth truth into their hearts and will be led by the Holy Spirit.[134] The Holy Spirit helps new believers, become a new creation born of the Spirit[135] and confirms that the believers belong to the

---

[131] John 14:26

[132] Titus 3:5; 2 Peter 1:4

[133] 1 Corinthians 6:19–20

[134] Romans 8:14

[135] 2 Corinthians 5:16-17

Lord and become an heir of God and joint heirs with Christ.[136] The Holy Spirit is not acting as just the influence that moves us to do certain things, but He is the one who prays through us and intercedes. Thus, believers feel comfortable when the Holy Spirit intercedes as Christ does.

As the Holy Spirit leads, the believers will be able to understand and apply the Scriptures in their daily[137] walks of life, where they will feel the love of God in their lives and fill their hearts with gratitude for things they did not know are revealed to them. When the believers feel weak and despair, the Holy Spirit will intercede for them[138] with the will of God living out in their lives and giving strength for them to overcome. Walking in Spirit, as commanded by Paul, written to Galatians, for they will not fall into the lust of the flesh;[139] thus, they will live for Christ to do God's will. They will be led by the Spirit and seek what is holy and righteous. As a result of the fruit in the Spirit, they will live a life worthy of, as followers of Christ, filled with love, joy, peace, longsuffering, kindness, goodness, faithfulness, gentleness, and self-control.[140] Those who are not led by the Spirit, or not of the Spirit, have not received the gift of salvation through Jesus Christ and reject Christ, where the Holy Spirit will be grieved.[141] The Holy Spirit will convict the believer to come before Christ and confess their sins thus the fellowship is restored between God and man.[142]

---

[136] Romans 8:15–17

[137] 1 Corinthians 2:12

[138] Romans 8:26–27

[139] Galatians 5:16

[140] Galatians 5:22-23

[141] Ephesians 4:30

[142] Romans 5:8

The Holy Spirit will lead believers and bring results of the fruits of the Holy Spirit in their lives. The old sinful life or nature, mentioned in Galatians 5:19-21, "sexual immorality, impurity, and debauchery; idolatry and witchcraft; hatred, discord, jealousy, fits of rage, selfish ambition, dissensions, factions, and envy; drunkenness, orgies, and the like," [143] will not be reflected in the believer's life. Our sinful nature will no longer reflect our lives; instead, the leading of the Holy Spirit will reflect His nature in our lives. But, still, believers battle the sinful flesh even in the new nature in Christ. [144] As believers, we will never conquer sinful nature, but the Holy Spirit's power is available. [145] We need to allow the Holy Spirit to produce more of His fruit in our lives that conquer the sinful nature.

At the same time, believers need clarification regarding the gift of speaking in tongues. There needs to be more clarity within the believers regarding why one needs the gift of speaking tongues, and for what purpose. The agreement of scripture is of great importance as it is a must for believers when they receive the gift as a real language that one would interpret, like it was in the early church, with purpose and communicable, not unclear words. [146] The purpose for the gift would be to communicate God's Word with a person of another language. [147] Paul spoke of this in 1 Corinthians 14:27-28, "If anyone speaks in a tongue, two—or at the most three—should speak, one at a time, and someone must interpret. If there is no interpreter, the speaker should keep quiet in

---

[143] New King James Version

[144] 2 Corinthians 5:17

[145] 2 Corinthians 5:17; Philippians 4:13

[146] 1 Corinthians 14:10

[147] Acts 2:6–12

the church and speak to himself and God."[148] Many practices in today's church constantly misuse the speaking of tongues that are not within the leading of the Holy Spirit and sovereignty of the Holy Spirit giving of the spiritual gifts.[149] Thus, speaking in a tongue should not be the focal point of experiencing the Holy Spirit in one's life, instead, seeks the fruit of the Holy Spirit reflected continually in one's life.

The Holy Spirit will continually work in our lives, even during the tribulations. Some misunderstand that the Holy Spirit will not be present, but He will be, and He will continually lead believers; of course, He will no longer restrain the growth of evil, unlike now and before.[150] They will be saved in the tribulation but endure persecution and receive comfort from the Holy Spirit. But, there will be a time when the work of the Holy Spirit will be removed.

No matter the time we live in or what we are doing currently, we must remember what the Holy Spirit is doing. We need to allow the Holy Spirit to guide[151], comfort[152], convict[153], teach[154], restrain sin, and give commands.[155] So, God's will in our lives will be fulfilled through our obedience to the leading of the Holy Spirit.

---

[148] New King James Version

[149] 1 Corinthians 12:11

[150] 2 Thessalonians 2:7-9

[151] Romans 8:14

[152] John 14:26

[153] John 16:8

[154] John 16:13

[155] Isaiah 59:19, Acts 8:29

Group Discussion

Leaders: Explain why it is important to know who the Holy Spirit is and what He is doing for them, and share your experience of how the Holy Spirit is leading you. Then, review the questions and answer by finding the reference bible verses.

1) Who was confronted by the Holy Spirit for lying to the Holy Spirit, and what was the punishment? Acts 5:3-4

2) Does the Holy Spirit possess a divine nature, such as omniscient and omnipresent? 1 Corinthians 2:10-11, Psalm 139:7-8

3) Was the Holy Spirit involved in creation? Genesis 1:2, Psalm 33:6, Job 26:13

4) What does it mean when one could grieve the Holy Spirit? Ephesians 4:30

5) Just like Christ, does the Holy Spirit intercede for us? How? Romans 8:26-27

6) Does the Holy Spirit act as a comforter and counselor like Jesus promised He would be? John 14:16, 15:26

7) Who did Jesus promise will come? John 14:26

8) Who gave life to man and other living creatures? Psalm 104:29-30

9) Why did God talk to Joshua as He is about to become a leader of the Israelites? Numbers 27:18

10) What was the difference between Saul and David, both being chosen by God to lead his people? 1 Samuel 10:9, 10, 14, 2 Samuel 23:2

11) What is the nature of the Holy Spirit? Titus 3:5, 2 Peter 1:4

12) Is the Believer's body like a temple that the Holy Spirit dwells in? 1 Corinthians 6:19-20

13) What does it mean when one is born of the Spirit? 2 Corinthians 5:16-17

14) When one is given the gift of speaking in one tongue, what did Paul speak of how it needs to be used? 1 Corinthians 14:27-28

15) What are the roles of the Holy Spirit? Romans 8:14, John 14:26, John 16:8, John 16:13, Isaiah 59:19, Acts 8:29

PART TWO:

LIVING A BALANCED LIFE KNOWING WHO GOD IS AND WHO WE ARE

CHAPTER 4

STEP 4, KNOWING OTHERS

What does Liberalism in Christianity propose? The Bible has errors.

The liberal theologian's theological difference creates such a gap that it could lead believers to false teachings that distort the true gospel and lead them to hell. Most liberal theologians are trying to interpret scripture to consolidate with the social norm, secular thinking, and science. Thus, they interpret the scripture their way and discredit the bible as having errors. For a quick example, they believe Genesis needs to be read as poetry or fantasy rather than literal. They find another example that frequently mentions that Moses did not write the Pentateuch. Thus, they propose that the scripture is not God-inspired, just a man's writing, which is a direct contradiction against Christian core doctrine.[156] They see errors or minor differences within the passages as an example of a man

---

[156] 2 Timothy 3:16-17

making a mistake. But they forget there are differences that do not contradict the passage's intention and meaning; finding archaeological evidence, relations, and history validates this truth.

No Miracles, No Hell, No Sinner

They do not believe in miracles such as the virgin birth[157], death on the cross, resurrection[158], or miracles Jesus performed during His ministry. They believe that if God does exist, which they do not, He will not punish them; for He is a loving God who will not judge for a man is good. Thus, there cannot be any place, such as hell. But, the scripture is very clear that Christ died to save us from sin[159] and proclaims that only through Him one could go to God.[160] Since they already discredit the bible, they could also discredit what is written in it. They focus on creating a scenario similar to secular modern thinking, where miracles should not be taken at face value but ignored.

Everything in the name of Love

Today, when we look at the world around us, we see love as a symbol of beacon and essential for society to become a better place. Love is not everything that happens in today's society. It is often ignored how much hate and evil exist within a man's wickedness, where man's depravity of sin cannot be ignored. A man cannot do what is good and love because they are sinners who need redemption.[161]

---

[157] Isaiah 7:14 and Luke 2

[158] Luke 24:6-7

[159] John 3:16

[160] John 14:6

[161] 2 Corinthians 5:7

Catholicism and Cults

Catholics

Why are there divisions between Roman Catholics and Christianity? The division between Roman Catholics and Christianity has continued for a long time, but the critical difference is its belief that faith alone in Christ is insufficient for salvation. We all know that the scripture is clear and that Christ alone brings salvation; as you accept, through grace, we receive salvation.[162] This claim by Christianity is not valid for the Roman Catholic Church, where they have added their tradition of the need to be baptized and receive the sacraments, abide by the decree of the Roman Catholic Church, and do the utmost works. All of this must be part of the life of believers. But does this reflect that all believers in the Roman Catholic Church put their genuine faith in Christ alone? Some genuinely place their faith in Christ, but they are blind to where they stay with the Church due to upbringings within the family traditions and with social gatherings of their peers.

Now, as we dive into further detail and examine the arguments presented, the apostles established the Roman Catholic church, proclaimed it the first true church, and brought the bible, and the Roman Catholic church stands as one rather than Protestants, with many denominations. These arguments are valid for the Roman Catholic Church, but let's examine it in detail. First, let's dive into the Roman Catholic Church's proposal, claiming to be the only first true church. Throughout the history of the Roman

---

[162] John 1:12, Ephesians 2:8-9

Catholic Church, we can see how much of their tradition was not built based on scripture. For example, the recognition of the pope, speaking to priests as opposed to God, requires infant baptism, and prayer to saints or Mary instead of Jesus. They have deviated so far from the original intent of the church that it is far from a Christ-following church and His word. God used the early church to canonize the Bible. Still, they forget God is sovereign. God is the one who inspires the writer under the instruction of God.[163] Without the reformation, we would never have known God's word personally and closely as we do today. Because only a selected few had access, the word of God was proclaimed through them. The Roman Catholic Church, like Pharisees and Sadducees[164], believes in suppression and oppression rather than being open to interpretation under the guidance of the Holy Spirit within the believers. They have suppressed those who question their teaching and tradition as heresy. They brought forth the judgment of death who disagreed with them. They also outcast those who speak not according to the tradition that the Church stands by. Within the denomination with Protestants, there is a minimum difference, but all stand with core doctrine, except for cults who have completely misinterpreted and taught false teaching.[165]

Mormons

Mormonism is associated with the Church of Jesus Christ of Latter-day Saints, found through Joseph Smith, Jr., through the vision and encounter with angels, and the discovery of miraculous records on plates of gold. He proclaimed to be a prophet, seer, and revelator. Through his death, Mormonism grew through the church of Latter-Day Saints and was well funded through a

---

[163] 2 Timothy 3:16-17

[164] Matthew 16:11-12

[165] Matthew 24:24

business empire and missionary outreach to the world. One needs to understand why it is crucial to understand the development of cultic groups outside of Christianity. They practice mission-mindedness, sincerity, dedication, and zealousness; they practice many Old and New Testament principles, including tithing to those in need if they are in the church. The Mormon church seems to follow fundamental Christian doctrine up to a certain level, but what they are declaring as truth is false, and claims that they are the true church through their interpretation of the scripture and its prophets and traditions are far from the Christian doctrine; they are evil in how they are standing against the truth.

The one consistency with cults is that they proclaim Christianity is wrong and all creeds are an abomination and corrupt; only truth exists within. Historians alike found that the basic untrustworthiness of the source for Joseph Smith was the glass lookers, "fortune tellers," and the various lawsuits of the assault, banking fraud, and following convictions. Also, the Book of Mormon fails the test as a new revelation of God, for there are serious doctrinal errors, such as of Jesus. In comparison, the core belief in Christianity is the doctrine of God, monotheistic, tribune God, God the Father, Son, Jesus Christ, and the Holy Spirit. However, the Mormon Church defines the doctrine of the Trinity as a belief in three separate gods, a belief in tritheism, and falling into polytheistic religion. Thus, they proclaimed Jesus Christ was to be a second god, created by Eloheim. In the theology of Mormonism, the Priesthood occupies a position of authority and greater importance.

Mormonism goes against Christ as a high priest, mediator, and intercessor in the presence of the Father. Some contradictions are internal and external, historical, theological, and scientific, which leads to the conclusion that it possesses an occultist background, which started from Joseph Smith as an occultist. One practice as an occultist is Ouija boards, fortune-telling, tarot cards, seances, palm reading, water witching, and witchcraft, which is very much aligned with Satanic activities. They have carefully redefined these activities as the perpetuity of spiritual gifts. Faith, repentance, and good works bring salvation in Mormonism and obedience to the LDS laws has been taught as their version of the gospel; there is no room for salvation by grace, nor through faith in Jesus Christ. The Mormon Church considers male church members above the age of twelve in correspondence to the Aaronic priesthood at the hands of John the Baptist, the Melchizedek Priesthood, to partake in serving as deacons. They are groomed from a young age to be brainwashed in their doctrine, not to question the authority within the LDS. They also want to avoid being called Mormons now to remove the bias that has been built around the term; thus, they want to be regarded as Christians or LDS. They are being deceitful to people by trying to market themselves as those who follow Jesus Christ, but that is not the case. As mentioned before, they follow a completely different Jesus. First, we need to be aware of the difference and share with those who do not know Jesus Christ so they will not get deceived by the Mormon Church.

Jehovah's Witness

It may not be familiar when one mentions Millim Dawn's movement, but when one mentions Jehovah witness tracks from Watchtower Bible and Tract Society, we are very familiar because of their fervent passion and focus on reaching people through outreach and tracks. They are the offspring of Millim Dawn's movement and they are cults. Now, why is that so different that they are considered cults? They deny the deity of Christ, salvation, the Trinity, and the Holy Spirit. Jehovah's Witnesses believe Jesus is a created being, such as Michael the archangel. With one difference, everything to do with Jesus' atonement work on the cross and the scriptures is direct contractions to Jehovah's Witness where Jesus is God.[166] Jehovah's Witnesses believe a combination of faith, good works, and obedience obtains salvation. A somewhat similar trait with all cults, where they are indirectly forcing people to follow their teachings by being obedient and doing good work for their cause. This directly contradicts the Bible, which declares salvation through faith to be received by grace.[167]

Judaism

Judaism, the origin, is rooted in divine revelation rather than pagan sources. Many have tried to attribute the influence of Zoroasim, but it is of Yahwistic faith. Judaism is defined as the religion and culture of Jewish people; civilization includes historical, social, and political dimensions in addition to religion. Judaism sees four pillars, God, Torah, the people of Israel, and the land of Israel. Jews held onto the Torah, bearers of God's word to the world, and stood in sharp contrast to their neighbors. One encounter, Rabbinic literal, presents insight into early Christian thought through a study of the Talmud, Mishnah or Oral Law, Midrash, and illustration.

First, one must know that the Israelites are chosen by God's sovereign plan in history to establish His covenant with Abraham. It is vital to recognize one's past to establish confidence about the future. But, the root of Israel's faith in God is somewhat neglected by Christians because Jews have rejected the Messiah, Jesus Christ. For Christians to fully understand, one must enter their world and become aware of their culture. Thus, Jewish scholars and Christians alike seek to understand Pauline's thoughts. Platonic thought, which is ancient Greek, and could easily influence the understanding of the Bible; for this reason, one must look at

---

[166] Acts 8:29

[167] Acts 8:29

Jews to understand the Bible entirely. Paul looked to Jews, and Christ as central to His teaching, preaching, and living; Jesus constituted the New Torah.

Meanwhile, Jews denied divine sonship and His return, thus rejecting His deity, resulting in unbelief in the promise and fulfillment of Messiah within Christ—the division with theological differences centered on Jesus and the outbreak of persecution against Christians. Meanwhile, the continuous persecution and ban between Jews and Christians eventually separated them. The first and second Jewish revolts was a decisive turning point from Judaism to Christianity, they led to anti-Judaism; from the second century to the present day, Church was essentially made up of gentiles, tied from its Jewish roots de-Judaized, versus the earliest church believers found the identity as part of Judaism. From Bible times to the present, Jews have been exiled and victims of hostility and hatred; out of all tribulation, Jews learn one thing, a quest for learning, where no one could ever take that away. The primary focus of education was to train one to seek lifelong knowledge of God and be obedient to the word.

The majority of Jews would proclaim Judaism teaches salvation by works of the Law; on the other hand, Christianity represents the grace of God. The Jews of Bible times did not simply think truth; they experienced truth; for that reason, the deeds are always more important than the creed, which one could say is very practical, more wanting to know what God wants one to do, works, verse describing God's essence, grace and mercy. The Jews make no distinction between the sacred and secular life, all God's domain, which Christians should model after.

Islam

Islam is a monotheistic religion focused on the teaching of Muhammad and the prophets. They followed the Quran, revealed

Muhammad and Hadith, acts or teachings of Muhammad, and believed that Muhammad was the final prophet after Abraham, Moses, and Jesus. Muslims are required to follow the Five Pillars of Islam, Shahada, the declaration of faith; Salat, the daily prayers performed five times a day; Zakat, the annual giving of one's income to the poor and needy; Sawm: fasting during the month of Ramadan, and Hajj, the pilgrimage to Mecca. When one recalls Allah's name, "no God but one," it is monotheistic but fundamentally different from Christianity or Judaism, Islam means submission. Because Allah has different characteristics from the Christian conception of God, the obvious one is not tribune. The Christian monotheistic God exists in three persons: the Father, the Son, and the Holy Spirit. The focus on Jesus is God registrants as blasphemy to the average Muslim. The similarity lies in the Abrahamic lineage, which teaches that God has sent messengers, angels, and humans to turn back to God. Holy Words are divine scripture as a guide; Satan is a deceiver and continually deceives. This may be a surprise; Islam teaches about Jesus, His virgin birth, performing miracles, and that Jesus is the Messiah and waiting on Him as Christians do somewhat. There are also significant differences, for Jesus is not God or the second person of the Trinity, and did not die on the cross. Also, the teaching of Islam is to follow and do what will please Allah and earn his favor; Sharia translates as "the way." But Jesus said, I'm the way, the truth, and the life; no one comes to the Father except through me.[168] Jesus is the way.

    Now, what is the core Islamic worldview? Humans should all submit to the sovereign will of God, who predestined the universe, humanity with the express purpose of worshiping him. To guide humanity, Allah sent prophets to lead them out of ignorance. Prophets who are divinely appointed leaders are unlike

---

[168] John 14:6

the Prophets in the God of Christianity. Allah gave humanity the final, perfected religion; thus, Islam is the culmination of Judaism, Christianity, and all other world religions. Islam is a deeply grounded form of altruism, a desire to please God to escape hell or obtain heaven. Thus, Muslims must live good lives and hope for God's merciful judgment. Also, following the Sharia is the way, which is the answer to humankind's ignorance; more than just Islamic law it provides peace and abundance of his blessings.

At the same time, many would hear words such as jihad over the media, extreme Muslims promoting the conquest, promoted by the sword, and "holy war," which was the case with early Islam, not like death the early Christians faced to spread the good news. But, the Koran also mentioned that they should pursue with grace with unbelievers; Jihad simply means striving. Jihad has four types: one's heart, one's tongue, one's hand, and a sword. Thus, we need to recognize and speak openly to the Muslims to share the true Jesus with them.

Buddhism

In common consensus with belief in Buddhism among followers is the Four Noble Truths: Suffering exists, Suffering arises from craving and attachment, and one can overcome Suffering. The path to the end of suffering is the Eightfold Path. The Eightfold Path is Right Understanding, Right intention, Right speech, Right action, Right livelihood, Right effort, Right mindfulness, and Right concentration. At the same time, Buddhism is confusing and puzzling due to being a combination of religion, philosophy, or both. A religion or philosophy depends on the region but it originated in ancient India, based on the teachings of the Buddha, Siddhartha Gautama. Mahayana Buddhists worship many deities and seek grace from a Buddha or bodhisattva. At the same time, Theravadin Buddhists are atheists, and Zen practitioners rely on self-effort in practicing me, focus and body position. Many

Buddhists believe suffering is part of life despite different traditions and practices. The goal is to end suffering and the cycle of death and rebirth by realizing the Four Noble Truths and cultivating the Eightfold Path, as mentioned above. Although somewhat contradictory, Buddhism depends on the region and tradition; one may believe in many deities or all practical purposes of atheists.

There is a definite contrast between Buddhism's origins compared to Christianity. The Buddha did not know the tribute to God; he was no more than a man, and no creator or divine being can help one achieve spiritual goals and promote lamps to oneself. On the other hand, Jesus said He was the world's light. Jesus promoted moral corruption as a fundamental human problem, sin. But, the Buddha taught that the desire for gratification of one's ends and ego is the root of all suffering. The knowledge enables one to become a Buddha, escape suffering, and ultimately reach the final truth: emptiness, ultimate reality Void, and nonexistence. But, Christians worship a suffering Jesus nailed to a cross and showed a way to conquer the suffering by embracing it with his help. The Buddhists and Christians agree on certain principles such as not stealing, not lying, not killing, sexual immorality, compassion, and sympathy. Still, differences are great in reality, such as no God but an illusion for Buddhists vs. Christians who believe in God, who is merciful and loving and offers eternal salvation. For Buddha, the ethical life is a provisional raft that takes one to another short of nirvana, is unnecessary, and no longer prevails. Earthly, existence is necessarily a lot of tears because as long as one remains in the cycle of life, death, and rebirth, suffering is inevitable, continually endless. For Christians, the distinction between right and wrong is part of reality and will persist into eternal life. Christians believe in the salvation that comes by not renouncing life in the world but trusting in Jesus and living out loving and committed.

New Age Religions

The New Age movement gained popularity in the early 1980s with a belief in universal spiritualities under the benefits of self-growth and the well-being of one's life. They are collections of many different beliefs and practices that are intertwined together, a combination of all religions and traditions. It is not Judaism, Christianity, Islam, Humanism, rationalism, atheism, or skepticism, but somehow, it's intertwined to form a movement of a New Age of self-actualization. Thus, it is an umbrella term for various people, organizations, events, practices, and ideas. They achieved their goals through positive thinking, personal development, and alternative spirituality. The ones involved are general optimists in the spiritual discovery who seek a New World Order, a one-world government where self-realized righteousness dwells.

The New World Order under humankind goes directly against believing in God and Christ's kingdom; instead, they seek their mystical utopia. They promote monism; we are one, and the idea that all is one contradicts a biblical view of God's creation as diverse. They also promote pantheism, a counterfeit God and humanity, promoting words such as energy, force, and consciousness; God is impersonal and amoral. Also, they seek to push reawakening to self, and rediscovery of the true, inner, and divine self, instead of repenting one's self to God. They are to create their reality, which is uprooted in any objective moral order, unlike unchanging moral character and will of a personal God. Of course, they believe in unlimited human potential and seek mastery of self and cosmos, knowledge of God, and power within. They also practice new-age channeling and believe in such masters from above, like UFOs. Religious Syncretism is practiced, which is a counterfeit religion.

The New Age is preoccupied with self, higher self, and true self; ignoring negatives and believing the love of God is equivalent to self-love. They believe poor self-esteem and unenlightened self-image are seen as the root cause of all our problems. But, they are ignoring the fundamental problem of humanity, sin. Sin is a rebellion against God, exemplified further by pride demonstrated throughout the generations of humankind. Pride always overestimates self, independence, and underestimation depends on God. Thus, one needs to go to God, not to justify oneself with good self-estimate, but to seek God and His word, which commends one to self-denial and self-control, not self-worship.

Group Discussion

Leaders: Explain why knowing what others believe in among us is important and being ready to share God's love. First of all, share what you know of. Then, review the questions and answers by finding the reference bible verses and reference pages in the book.

1. The liberal theologians treat scripture as not God-inspired, just a man's writing, where there are errors or minor differences. What does the Christian core doctrine believe? 2 Timothy 3:16-17

2. The liberal theologians do not believe in miracles such as virgin birth, death on the cross, and resurrection, but what does the bible mention? Isaiah 7:14, Luke 2, Luke 24:6-7

3. The liberal theologians continually deny how loving God is by interpreting completely different love, what is God's true love and mercy as He sent Christ to die on the cross? John 3:16-17

4. The Catholics believe tradition, work, and faith are sufficient for salvation. But what does the bible say about salvation? John 1:12, Ephesians 2:8-9

5. What does the Roman Catholic Church try to do with those who do not believe in their teaching, like the Pharisees and Sadducees? Isaiah 10:1-12:6

6. Why is it important to watch out for false teachers and prophets? Matthew 24:24

7. The Mormon Church believes in tritheism; what does that mean? Refer to page 44-45.

8. What did Joseph Smith proclaim as a sign that he received God's revelation? Refer to page 44-45.

9. What do Jehovah's witnesses believe Jesus is? Refer to page 46.

10. What do Jehovah's Witnesses focus on? Refer to page 46.

11. What did Jews deny of Christ? Refer to page 46-47.

12. What does Islam teach? Refer to page 48-49.

13. What are the five pillars of Islam? Refer to page 48-49.

14. Does Islam teach about Jesus? Yes, then of what? Refer to page 48-49.

15. What is the Islamic worldview? Refer to page 48-49.

16. What are the four noble truths that Buddhism believes in? Refer to page 49-50.

17. How is Buddhism different from Christianity? Refer to page 49-50.

18. What do the new age religions have in common? Refer to page 51.

CHAPTER 5
STEP 5, LIVING AS A GOD'S CHILD

Old Identity

We are all sinners. Do you agree with this statement? When someone calls us sinners, what are our responses? It depends on where we are in our relationship with God. We consider sinners immoral, evil, or wicked, which is all true. But, in the scripture, the Greek translation of a sinner is one who demonstrates ignorance or misses the goal or purpose. Thus, we are sinners who miss God's purpose. The scripture is unambiguous: we all fall short of the glory of God.[169] We inherited the sins of disobedience from the beginning[170], original sin from Adam and Eve's failure under the temptation of Satan. But, the world foolishly tries to disguise sinfulness as humanism, the belief in human good and not having a sinful nature. The scripture states that not just humans fall into sin, but the angel, Lucifer, whom God created, falls into sin and rebels

---

[169] Romans 3:23

[170] Romans 5:12-14

against God to be greater than God. [171] God already had a plan when Adam and Eve fell, but they had to bear the consequences of their sin and were kicked out of the Garden of Eden, a place where they never had to experience death; now, they must face death. Thus, looking at Adam and Eve's actions validates that the human condition is deceitful and beyond cure. [172]

But God had a redemption plan through His Son already in motion. God's love for sinners is demonstrated and shown through paying for the wage of sin through His Son.[173] We all could identify the broken state of our relationship with God when we were living in sin as sinners[174] and slaves to sin. [175] We were bound to face the judgment of God[176], death, and destruction. [177] Regardless of good works, we are still sinners at the end of the day and need to deal with this corrupt nature.

The Jewish leaders were highly regarded by people for their knowledge on the Law of God and also for being able to live according to the Law of God and thus rejected many as sinners, such as Gentiles[178], those who broke the law and did not keep the tradition, committed crimes[179], and bad reputable women.[180] But,

---

[171] Isaiah 14:12-15

[172] Jeremiah 17:9

[173] Romans 5:8

[174] 1 John 3:4

[175] John 8:34

[176] Jude 1:14–15

[177] Ezekiel 18:20; James 1:5

[178] Galatians 2:15

[179] Luke 15:2

[180] Luke 7:37

Jesus Christ changed the perception of sinners. He came for the sinner, and heaven will rejoice if one sinner repents. [181] We all know that Jesus knew who needed His help; very clearly, He wanted those who were lost and sick[182] to come before Him, restoring the broken and mended relationship brings joy to the Lord[183], and heaven rejoices. [184] Thus, there can be only hope for sinners who repent.

We know our sinful nature is from Adam and the beginning, the inherited sin passed on from conception. [185] Thus, bringing forth the question of what Imputed sin is "to take something that belongs to someone and credit it to another's account." All are destined to be accountable for their sin, which is subject to death, not because they have disobeyed the law but because of their own inherited sin. Through the account of Christ, who paid for sin through His death on the cross, God imputed the sins of believers. But, even though Christ imputed the sin of believers, He was still sinless, with no inherited sin. He was not a sinner and never was a sinner. Thus, there can be only His righteousness, which is why Christ can bear all the sins of the believers. [186]

Since we have inherited a sinful nature, we will continually commit personal sins, which we must deal with on a personal level. We are redeemed through God's grace and faith in Christ[187] and

---

[181] Luke 15:7,10

[182] Mark 2:17

[183] Luke 15:7

[184] Luke 15:10

[185] Psalm 51:5

[186] 2 Corinthians 5:21

[187] Ephesians 1:7

freed from eternal judgment.[188] Also, God equips one to receive help from the Holy Spirit to resist the temptation of sin[189], and if we fall, we could go to God for His forgiveness, and He will cleanse us.[190] Many have failed to renew their relationship with God through their disobedience to God. They followed their ways and the world's ways and were spiritually blinded.

Adam and Eve were deceived and blinded by Satan's temptation, where they compromised their trust in God and consumed the forbidden fruit. They lost what they truly were blessed with. Yet, God still demonstrated His grace by providing them with cover by killing animals once they recognized that they were naked. This killing of animals symbolizes Christ's sacrifice as the animals were sacrificed to cover Adam and Eve's shame. Adam's son, Cain, was jealous of Abel, his brothers' offering accepted by God. So, he killed his brother and denied God by responding to Him, Am I my brother's keeper?[191] God let him live as he asked for mercy. Jacob was deceitful to his brother Esau, as he was seeking a blessing from his father. He pretended to be his brother and deceived his faith to receive the blessing.[192]

Meanwhile, Esau, his foolishness, deceived by his brother over the bowl of soup, could not overcome his hunger and lost his blessing, which he was his to start with. God still blesses Jacob by showing mercy, and Esau continually receives God's provision. God chose Saul to become the first king of God's people, the Israelites. But, when Saul starts becoming jealous of David and

---

[188] Revelation 20:11-15

[189] Romans 8:9-11

[190] 1 John 1:9

[191] Genesis 4:9

[192] Genesis 27:1-29

tries to murder David, he disobeys God, and the spirit of God leaves him. He did not heed God's prophets' word but went to the medium. Jealousy is the wrong place to receive peace.

Solomon has achieved so much from a young age and was called wise. But, over the years, he compromised his faith in God. Wives from a foreign land who worshiped idols and foreign gods influenced him. He knew what he should have done, but he forsakes the God who blessed him.

Samson was a man of great strength, blessed by God and raised by righteous parents. But, he fell into the temptation of Delilah, who was setting him up to be trapped, where he lost the power from his hair, which was instructed not to be cut by God. He lost everything he had because he was influenced by sexual temptation. Meanwhile, Jesus shares the parable with the disciples regarding the Prodigal Son. It is a story about a young man with a wealthy and good father, but left him so he could enjoy his life. So, he got his portion of the inheritance and lived a life of partying and foolishness. One day, he lost all his money, and looking back on his stay in his father's place, he realized that he had to go back, work as a servant, not as a son, and be better. He returned, and his father celebrated his return with a welcome-back party. God is always welcoming us with open arms. But, we are like a prodigal son and could be one if we look to the wrong side of the world when we start seeking what the world offers to us. We want to try what the world offers to enjoy at all costs: the lies that Satan whispers to all of us to make us fall. There is nothing wrong with enjoying what God created and allowed us to. But, like the Prodigal Son, we could be foolish to understand the love and mercy of God until it is too late. Also, at the same time, we could be another brother filled with jealousy, resentful of the father's action toward the return of their brother. We could be complainers, not knowing how our Father was always faithful.

Pharisees and Sadducees were the elite and leaders during Jesus' ministry. But they hated Jesus so much for speaking the truth of God and who He is to them. They were filled with hate and evil in their hearts. Doubting Thomas, we all know him from when he had to confirm the resurrection of Jesus by touching his hands. We could all doubt Christ or doubt God just because we feel alone. We see in the scripture how many have fallen into temptation, and we are not prone to the temptation of this world. Do we see ourselves through some mentioned? We need to remove the old self from our DNA, and transform by the grace of God.

New Identity

John 3:16-17 mentions, "For God so loved the world that He gave his one and only Son, that whoever believes in him shall not perish but have eternal life. For God did not send his Son into the world to condemn the world, but to save the world through him."[193] Thus, we receive a new identity that comes from accepting Christ into our hearts. We are new creations in Christ.[194] We used to be in the world, but now, in Christ. So, everything about us changed once and for all. We don't belong to the world or our old selves. We cannot be of the world when we are in the world. We are following Him and His example, which will be demonstrated and taught through His teaching. We are to seek righteousness, godliness, faith, love, patience, and gentleness.[195]

Even though we live in this world, we are no longer citizens of this world, but we are citizens of God's kingdom. We should not focus on this world but on the things above.[196] As one

---

[193] New King James Version

[194] 2 Corinthians 5:17

[195] 1 Timothy 6:9-11, Romans 6:13

[196] Colossians 3:2

knows that Christ began a good work[197], a child of God should abide by His word by holding to His deliverance. We should not be afraid or live in fear. [198]

Many in the scripture walked righteously even under the corruption, wickedness, and struggles that exist as a follower of God. They demonstrated faith over and over by putting their trust in God. God always delivers the promised plan for them. For instance, Noah found favor in the sight of God in times of tribulation and lived in a wicked and evil world. He did not compromise his faith in God and put his trust in Him. We must build ourselves like Noah, as we live in a corrupt and evil world. Also, Moses leads his people out of Egypt under the bondage of sin. He was not perfect, but he trusted God to use him continually. He did something impossible within, but God was there for him and walked with him. Even though Moses was not perfect, God was with him. We must build our faith continually by trusting God that He is with us and will lead us from the bondage of sin and temptation of this world. David was not afraid of a Philippine Giant; he knew that God would be there for him, and he knew what he needed to do: act. We need to act when God calls us to, with the confidence and boldness of him.

Peter was not afraid to speak the truth and knew what was important to him. Sometimes, he spoke too harshly or bluntly, but his heart was always toward Christ. When we are in faith and relationship with Christ, we always need not be afraid to speak Christ's truth. Paul, one who spoke boldly of Jesus, once he encountered Jesus, the transformation was instant and powerful; Paul changed completely to serve Christ and knew that he was wrong. He never faltered after the encounter he had. He preached

---

[197] Philippians 1:6

[198] Colossians 1:2, 1 Peter 3:14

under persecution.

Transformation

We can not leave out Paul, who was transformed completely by and for Christ. But before the encounters with Jesus, Paul, Saul of Tarsus, a Jew from the tribe of Benjamin[199], who has Roman citizenship, was known to be the one who notoriously went after the followers of Jesus Christ for blaspheming God's name. Paul followed the Law of Moses as a Pharisee. [200]

At a young age, from adulthood, he was taught by Gamaliel, learned and mastered all required to become a Pharisee, learning God's law[201], and he had a zeal and passion for God's word to keep and live by. For this reason, he was eager to go after the Christians and eliminate them from the public.[202] The Christians feared him and his action against them. But, when Jesus met him on the road to Damascus, there could be only one way that Paul could go forward. Jesus spoke to him, why are you persecuting me? I am Jesus. He heard, "Saul, Saul, why are you persecuting me?" He replied, "Who are you, Lord?" Jesus answered directly and clearly, "I am Jesus, whom you are persecuting"[203]—transformation, blinded by the light, where he was instructed to go to Ananias. Ananias resists taking him in, but the Lord tells Ananias he will be a vessel God uses.[204] Through laying of his hands and through prayer, Saul received the Holy Spirit; eyesight

---

[199] Philippians 3:5-6

[200] Acts 22:22-29

[201] Acts 22:3

[202] Acts 8:3

[203] Acts 9:4–5

[204] Acts 9:1-22

healed, was baptized[205], and started proclaiming that Jesus is the Son of God. [206]

Paul took many journeys to the Gentiles, where they started hearing the gospel, and Paul set up the churches. His purpose after the encounter with Jesus was to share about Christ with Gentiles, the Roman world, through his sacrifice and suffering[207], until the end, facing a martyr's death in Rome.

When one meets Jesus, there is no turning back to old ways. But, there are only new ways where Jesus will be leading. For Paul, it was clear that God had prepared him to share the gospel with Gentiles. He was not perfect or a saint; he had done wrong to many believers. But God brought forth him as a disciple to share the gospel and wash his past away through the blood of Jesus Christ.

The transformation in our lives requires a complete turnaround, not little by little. Sometimes, that is an excuse we make ourselves to cover our weakness and lack of faith in God. When we are in front of the cross path, where God is there, there is only one way: through Jesus Christ, we know that what we knew in the past was the lies of this world. Our eyes are open wide to see who Jesus is. Paul showed us commitment from the start to the end of his life.[208] He knew his purpose.[209]

Relationship with God as Heavenly Father

---

[205] Acts 9:18

[206] Acts 9:20

[207] 2 Corinthians 11:24-28

[208] Philippians 1:12-14

[209] Acts 16:22-25, Philippians 4:11-13

We did not know what it meant to be in love or the presence of God, because we were blinded by the word and prince of this world, Satan.[210] In Romans 9:8 says that "That is, those who are the children of the flesh, these are not the children of God; but the children of the promise are counted as the seed."[211] We need to know that we are born with sin, which separates us from God and aligns with Satan, God's enemy; thus, we are far from being born as God's children.[212] Jesus said to them, "If God were your Father, you would love Me, for I proceeded forth and came from God; nor have I come of Myself, but He sent Me."[213] The fact is that those who are not saved are not children of God.[214] Children of the devil[215] practice sinning. Still, Jesus came to stop the work of the devil to let us know that we are bought with price.[216] As the children of God, we are new creations in Christ,[217] led by the Holy Spirit.

    Let's clarify: We are no longer sinners as we are identified with Christ; we are entering God's big family. We have now mended our relationship with God, broken through Christ. We can call our heavenly father now; we are adopted into the family of God through Christ. We have a relationship that is stronger than family.[218] We have a Father who loves us and who will be there for

---

[210] James 4:4, 1 John 3:8

[211] New King James Version

[212] James 4:4; 1 John 3:8

[213] John 8:42

[214] 1 John 3:10

[215] John 8:44

[216] 1 John 3:8

[217] 2 Corinthians 5:17

[218] Matthew 10:35-37

us[219], Friend[220], Heirs[221], Confidence[222], Wisdom and guidance.[223]

God's great love takes the initiative to make us the children of God. This plan of our heavenly Father's love amazed John the apostle and wrote in 1 John 3:1: "Behold what manner of love the Father has bestowed on us, that we should be called children of God! Therefore the world does not know us, because it did not know Him."[224] Even though we experience God's goodness, we have only limited knowledge of what it means to be children of God under what is being revealed to us in 1 John 3:2-3: "Beloved, now we are children of God; and it has not yet been revealed what we shall be, but we know that when He is revealed, we shall be like Him, for we shall see Him as He is. And everyone who has this hope in Him purifies himself, just as He is pure."[225]

In the future, when we see Jesus, our understanding of what it means to be children of God will be revealed fully.[226] Yet, John explained, even a simple understanding of our status, will renew our lives to live more holy and make us live pure.[227] Also, it reminded us of how good it is to be children of God since we have a new nature now "and that you put on the new man which was

---

[219] Romans 8:15-16

[220] John 15:15

[221] Galatians 3:29

[222] Hebrews 4:16

[223] James 1:5

[224] New King James Version

[225] New King James Version

[226] 2 Corinthians 3:18

[227] 1 John 3:9–10

created according to God, in true righteousness and holiness."[228]

    We need to understand that our works do not bring salvation that exists within God. We are chosen and adopted into God's family; undeserving and rebellious as we are, he picked us up and showed his love to us. God's grace and mercy are demonstrated in Ephesians 1:5-6: "adopted as his sons through Jesus Christ, in accordance with his pleasure and will—to the praise of his glorious grace, which he has freely given us in the One he loves."[229] We have a good father who cares and loves us, and he will provide all our needs. Thus, we need to see only His love through the gift he gave us through Jesus' blood. We are all called through putting faith in Christ Jesus by confessing our sins and trust in Him, we are no longer slaves but sons and daughters, heirs of God through Christ.[230] The purpose set before us changed once we became children of God. We are to follow Christ's example and mature in trusting God.[231] Now, as children of God, we are to inherit the kingdom of God[232] and be blessed with spiritual and earthly blessings within God's provision. We will receive peace and the indwelling of the Holy Spirit[233], which will encourage us to live and follow God to know His everlasting love.

Sanctification, Glorification

What does it mean to sanctify? We don't hear this word too often in everyday conversations between believers. But we all know what

---

[228] Ephesians 4:24

[229] New King James Version

[230] Galatians 4:4-7

[231] Romans 8:29

[232] Matthew 25:34

[233] Ephesians 1:13-14

it means: maturing and transforming in Christ. First, we must understand what sanctification means: to set apart for special use and make a person holy. God wants all of us to be sanctified, and it is His will.[234] Meanwhile, we need first to understand what our Lord Jesus Christ has taught us about sanctification. As Jesus prays for disciples, he prays to the Father by asking the disciples to be sanctified by the truth that comes from the word of God and set apart from the world for God.[235] Those who are in faith will grow in the wisdom of God[236] and grow in faith as they seek to sanctify before God. God will continually make the believers grow in faith because he has started a good work in them till the day of Christ.[237] God's word continually reminds us that he is holy and expects us to seek holiness in all our actions.[238] We know it cannot be done overnight, but through taking each step of obedience, we will be sanctified, and be more like Christ.[239]

There can be only fruit of the spirit to those who are being sanctified.[240] Meanwhile, the Holy Spirit works in us to be more like Christ[241] and demonstrate gentleness of Christ to others. Gentleness, also translated as "meekness," does not mean weakness but demonstrates humility and thankfulness toward God, not anger or a desire for revenge. It takes strength to be truly gentle.

---

[234] 1 Thessalonians 4:3

[235] John 17:6-7, John 17:17

[236] 1 Corinthians 1:30

[237] Philippians 1:6

[238] 1 Peter 1:15

[239] Hebrew 10:14

[240] Galatians 5:22-23

[241] Ephesians 4:14-16

7 Steps to a Grace-Filled Life Right Now

God wants us to give Him control of our lives, not fall in our understanding. We need to rely on the Holy Spirit, knowing that human power has limits. We need to be gentle, but control under guidance becomes a powerful tool for doing God's work. Everything we do has meaning, and all actions have consequences to follow, such as communication with others influences to build up or destroy. Gentleness channels that power within, amplified with God's will and recognition of God's way and things.[242] It is to accept God's worldview, not the worldview or our views. God knows of the past, present, and future[243]; God understands more than we possibly would know.[244]

In Galatians 5:22-23, "But the fruit of the Spirit is love, joy, peace, longsuffering, kindness, goodness, faithfulness, gentleness, self-control. Against such, there is no law." [245] When filled with the Spirit's fruit of gentleness, we encourage and lead others easily instead of arguing, for sharing goodness is more important than our ego or pride.[246] Thus, we will forgive and preach the good news. [247] For example, John the Baptist demonstrated his humbleness and gentleness as he faced the greater one by speaking in John 3:30 "He must increase, but I must decrease." [248] Even though John the Baptist was well known first, and he spoke of repentance with conviction and passion to Jews. He stands for holiness and righteousness from everyone that he

---

[242] Isaiah 55:9

[243] 1 John 3:20

[244] Psalm 44:21

[245] New King James Version

[246] 2 Timothy 2:24-25

[247] Philippians 1:15-18

[248] New King James Version

encounters and until death. Jesus also demonstrated His gentleness, a king coming on a donkey, humble yet fulfilling the prophecy. They both demonstrated gentleness that cannot be pushed over, firm yet loving and encouraging.

Love cannot be forced or coerced. We cannot truly love God without the guidance of the Holy Spirit; as we experience the love of God, we realize more of God's love in our lives. Because we witnessed first what love is from God. God demonstrated His love through the sacrifice made by His Son, Jesus Christ, on the cross[249] so we will be saved and have eternal life. It is a choice that God made for us to be saved. It is a choice to think of others first. [250] God demonstrated love, agape love.

In Mark 12:30-31 states: "And you shall love the Lord your God with all your heart, with all your soul, with all your mind, and with all your strength.' This is the first commandment. And the second, like it, is this: 'You shall love your neighbor as yourself.' There is no other commandment greater than these."[251] Thus, As God's children, we are created with His nature, and the Holy Spirit will lead and empower us to experience His love and share His love with others as we mature in faith. The relationship with one another and the relationship with God are keys to truly living in peace as God's mature children. Why? Because we struggle in life with conflicts with others and God, things we seek do not come true. Paul knew that we would face suffering, persecution, or trials; thus, he recommends in 2 Corinthians 13:11, "Live in peace."[252] At the same time, it is tough to experience peace when the struggle is

---

[249] Philippians 2:3

[250] New King James Version

[251] New King James Version

[252] New King James Version

too great. God gives peace, and only His peace will provide us with the perseverance that comes from having a deeper relationship with God.

The struggle continues as long as we are in this world, for sin and principalities of this world will make us live in fear and despair. We need to know that we are equipped with the power that comes from God, where we will be in peace even though spiritual battle persists; need to know Jesus Christ is the prince of peace [253], and he won the battle, and he will declare the judgment once he returns. Thus, we need to be in the presence of God.[254]

We are to be the peacemaker, for we are chosen to be His children.[255] As the one who provides peace, we should not be anxious about anything and need to demonstrate in our lives how we are experiencing peace amid trial as well by being in prayer and supplication. We need to allow our hearts to be ruled by the peace of Christ and always be thankful, for we are part of God's family.[256] Thus, we will harvest the rightness in our lives, which is sown in peace.[257] We need not seek the passions of foolishness but seek righteousness with a pure heart.[258] Because those who seek foolishness are wicked there is no peace for them.[259]

God knows what is best for us, and the Holy Spirit will guide us; thus, a process in which we will prevail with God's love

---

[253] Isaiah 9:6

[254] Ephesians 2:11-18

[255] Matthew 5:9

[256] Colossians 3:15

[257] James 3:18

[258] 2 Timothy 2:22

[259] Isaiah 48:22

from the wicked and unrighteousness of this world. When we come into faith, we are justified by the blood of Jesus Christ and saved by God's grace. Sanctification is more like a process in which believers mature and grow in faith through the continual renewal of understanding God's holiness.

Group Discussion

Leaders: Explain the importance of knowing who we are to God as children of God. First of all, share your thoughts and your relationship with God. Then, review the questions and answers by finding the reference bible verses and reference pages in the book.

1. Why do we fall short of the glory of God? Romans 3:23, Romans 5:12-14

7 Steps to a Grace-Filled Life Right Now

2. How did Lucifer end up rebelling against God? Isaiah 14:12-15

3. How is the condition of mankind's heart? Jeremiah 17:9

4. Why is mankind destined to face the judgment of God? Jude 1:14–15

5. Who could bear all the sins of the believer? 2 Corinthians 5:21

6. Who do we have to put our faith in and accept the grace of God? Ephesians 1:7

7. Who is our helper to resist the temptation of sin? Romans 8:9-11

8. What does it mean to be saved by the blood of Jesus Christ? John 3:16-17

9. What do we need to seek in our lives as we put our faith in Jesus Christ? 1 Timothy 6:9-11, Romans 6:13

10. What do we need to focus on after knowing the truth of Jesus Christ? Colossians 3:2

11. What does God's word say about not living in fear? Colossians 1:2, 1 Peter 3:14

12. Who is Paul, and how did he transform? Philippians 3:5-6, Acts 22:22-29

13. Paul knew his purpose. Do we know our purpose? Philippians 1:12-14, Acts 16:22-25, Philippians 4:11-13

14. Who is the prince of this world? James 4:4, 1 John 3:8

15. Who do we belong to if we do not know God? 1 John 3:10, John 8:44

16. When we come to know God through Jesus Christ, we belong

to whom and what kind of relationship do we have with God and others who are in faith? Matthew 10:35-37

17. What kind of life should we live as children of God? 1 John 3:9-10

18. Did God demonstrate His grace and mercy through Jesus Christ toward us? Ephesians 1:5-6

19. What does it mean when one is sanctified by the truth? John 17:6-7, John 17:17

20. What does God expect us to do as we seek Him? 1 Peter 1:15

21. What is the fruit of the Spirit? Galatians 5:22-23

22. How did John the Baptist demonstrate his humbleness? John 3:30

23. How is one supposed to love God? Mark 12:30-31

24. How are we supposed to overcome the struggles of this world? Ephesians 2, Hebrews 11:6, Jeremiah 29:13

7 Steps to a Grace-Filled Life Right Now

CHAPTER 6
STEP 6, LIVING AS A GOOD STEWARD

God's plan as a steward

In Genesis, God created the earth and instructed Adam and Eve to enjoy the blessing from God. God himself demonstrated firsthand what it means to be working. "In the beginning, God created the heavens and the earth."[260] For the creation of mankind, He created in His image[261], demonstrated His closeness, and thus we are to reflect on Him as a source of knowledge and wisdom. God wants His creation to multiply, be fruitful, and become a steward of His creation.[262]

God's word reminds us throughout creation; throughout the scripture, that there can not be any doubt. God is very clear

---

[260] Genesis 1:1

[261] Genesis 1:27

[262] Genesis 1:28

about how one needs to know God to be a good steward. We came into faith through God's love[263] and His provision. Thus, when we start thinking away from His good plan that is filled with His love and start seeking money, which is the root of all kind of evil[264], that will destroy God's intention and plan, for this reason, we need to understand the biblical stewardship that will guard our hearts to not fall into the world's traps. We are all called to be fellow workers to build God's kingdom[265], and we need to allow God to show us the way.

God leads because He is the creator and owns everything, for it's all His creation. God decided to use us to bless us as we learn of His love by becoming a good steward of His creation. We cannot limit ourselves to only seeking material things but must also seek spiritual elements where we use our gifts and talents to promote Him and give Him glory so more will come into faith. We are called to join in with God to fulfill His plan and eternal plan for us. He gives us the gift of using our lives to know His love and faithfulness. All our lives need to center on being who we are, a steward. We use the word steward, which means manager, guardian, and administrator.

We could see how Jesus wants us to know what it means to do God's work. For example, let's look at the parable of the worker. The landowner goes out in the morning and hires the laborers based on the needs of the hours; he hires them in the third hour, sixth, and ninth hour, and then, at the eleventh hour, he goes out and hires more workers again. But, when the time came for pay, the one who came last got the same amount as the ones hired first. As a result, those who were hired earlier in the day

---

[263] John 3:16-17

[264] 1 Timothy 6:10

[265] 1 Corinthians 3:9

complained to the landowner. Still, he simply responded, "Take what is yours and go away, for I wish to give the same to the last man." (Matthew 20:1-16) [266] We need to know that when we are serving God, it is God who called us, and he will be just and fair, for he has given us what we deserve. Thus, we can not allow ourselves to calculate what God gives or not; we just need to be faithful in what God calls us to do all the time.

Now, when we look at the parable of a sower[267], we can see the principle of how important it is where one needs to sow. When one sows in the wayside, stony place, and thorns, it will all perish and cannot yield crop. Of course, Jesus is speaking about those denying the gospel, Pharisees, and religious leaders. Here, a good soil, those who are ready to listen and obey God's word and live to witness to others will be fruitful. There is a practical lesson that we could pick up here: it is important to sow in good soil so one does not waste time and effort. It is about how one needs to recognize God's plan and be attentive to what he is leading us to do. Sometimes, we could pull away from things that will be meaningless and fruitless.

Jesus teaches them again using the Parable, the Parable of the Talents; the owner gave five talents, two talents, and one talent, and told them to use their talents before leaving for a long trip. When he came back and asked for the results of those with five talents and two talents, they came back with ten and four talents, doubling their talents. While the one that got one talent just came up with one talent and did not do anything with it. The owner praised those who doubled their talents. But, with the one talent, he called him a wicked and lazy servant for not doing anything. So, the owner took away what he had and gave it to the ten and four

---

[266] Matthew 20:1-16

[267] Matthew 13:3-9

talents.[268] We could learn from here how God builds accountability in what He entrusted with His servants, and His people, which are us. We cannot ignore the calls that God has made in our lives to make a difference. We cannot ignore what God gave us to use, whether it is gifts, skills, talents, or financial blessings. In this context, it is to please God by being a good steward. But there are times when we are not good stewards. For example, if one were to hastily invest and lose everything because they did not follow God's principle and take the time to receive His wisdom. This thinking has some validity, but it is only sometimes true that one may take risks and lose everything. But it all depends on the condition of the heart, who it is for, and why it is done.

    Satan tempts and uses the things of this world to make us fail to be good stewards of God's entrusted resources. This is often due to our failure to manage properly. The materialism that we know brings obsession that affects Christians negatively. The temptation of materialism could instantly bring down the principles of being a good steward of managing finances. Because pursing obsession often replaces God and following His principles. God instructs all to love Him more than anything[269], where complete attention is given to Him. Thus, if our eyes are not focused on Him, we are turning our eyes to the idols of this world. The idols of this world, such as greed and jealousy, lead to seeking of wealth[270] instead of seeking God's kingdom.[271] There can not be satisfaction with wealth obtained[272], as it leads to the meaninglessness that is filled with vanity without God in one's life.

---

[268] Matthew 25:14-30

[269] Deuteronomy 6:5

[270] Ecclesiastes 5:10

[271] Matthew 6:33

[272] Ecclesiastes 5:10

This is the reason why one can not be satisfied with both money and God. [273] Now, there needs to be a proper understanding of wealth here. Wealth itself, or money, is neutral. Still, when money starts controlling, it becomes the root of all evil. [274] For example, purchasing material things without balance and acting upon their greed, basically doing all within their power to possess or have something.

 Jesus spoke to His disciples, teaching them how hard it is for a rich man to enter the kingdom of God. [275] Why? Because when one has everything, there is no reason to trust God. They could trust in what they have. This is the very reason that everyone is trying to build their wealth. Thus, they will not join the kingdom of God, for they put their trust in this earthly kingdom. We could see how where one puts their trust matters so much in Matthew 6:24, "No one can serve two masters; for either he will hate the one and love the other, or else he will be loyal to the one and despise the other. You cannot serve God and mammon"[276], it's very clear that one needs to choose one. One cannot live a compromised life. But, many put their faith in both. There can be only one; putting faith in God is the right path and way to live, building the treasure not in this world but in heaven.[277] Also, to overcome temptation, one needs to keep life free from the love of money and be content with what one has[278], then, God will continually be there and deliver them out of their temptations.

---

[273] Luke 16:13

[274] 1 Timothy 6:10

[275] Matthew 19:23

[276] New King James Version

[277] Matthew 6:19

[278] Hebrews 13:5

We need to ask for the Holy Spirit's leading; through His leading, we gain strength, inspiration, growth, and maturity, where our hearts will be in the right place so we can do what is right. Without the guidance of the Holy Spirit, we will quickly realize that our labor means nothing and thus experience fruitlessness. Biblical stewardship requires our practical and spiritual obedience, where we give our control over to God and put our trust in His leadership.

Now that we understand the principle of God's intent, we can apply ourselves to be good stewards of His creation. First, we need to understand the principle and the resources God gives in order to manage well; thus, money comes into the discussion from both worldview and Christian perspectives. Secondly, we need to understand how everything is interconnected between money, giving, tithing, and ministry, not just in the Old Testament but also in the New Testament, and even in modern times where we live.

The Views on Money, Giving, and Tithing

Depending on who one talks to, their views on money may vary because it is a spectrum based on a value system developed over one's life. Only some have seriously considered money as something other than the reason to make enough to live or survive. But, looking deep into one's life tells of one's values, such as how much one saves, spends, and to whom one gives. One's life story could be told by how they have earned and spent over time. Western culture values possessions that money can buy, not necessarily a love of money but entrapped in what money can do for oneself. Also, there are different distractions, not just culture but through various media platforms that lead us to believe that we need something. This material item will fulfill us or, at the very least, give us some form of happiness, although it is temporary. Thus, the Christian life is not immune but influenced strongly and requires the right principle and understanding of money biblically, as the scripture teaches.

Jesus talked so much about money; the parables he mentioned deal with money and possession and how to handle it accordingly. Jesus spoke on this more than any other subject and showed the importance of it; even the bible offers 2350 verses on money and possession, 500 verses on prayer, and less than 500 verses on faith. Understanding the principle of money and its application plays a crucial role in living in the freedom that comes from Christ. Many agree, everyone needs to work to earn money to provide for their needs, and others. Thus, many spend time on furthering their knowledge on how to save, invest, and spend appropriately. If one holds on to the money and misuses it, these actions will directly compete with the Lord. The secular society continually reminds one that God has no place in handling money; happiness comes from being able to afford one's desired standard of living. But, the scripture reminds us to follow the principles of handling money, which will build our life in Christ and teach us to live with contentment in all circumstances.

The sum of mishandling of finance through the accumulation of debts slowly through the years could result in anxiety and depression, and most do not realize this until they reach the tipping point where they cannot handle it anymore. The accumulation of debt in today's society more often than not, comes from a credit card with high interest. In most cases, one spends more than their earned income, and this debt is liable. This liability goes far beyond the burden of finances; it touches every aspect of life, and can negatively affect their relationship not only with God, but others.

Financial responsibility is essential in our society, especially among God's people and the Lord's activities. His people must remember that money only serves us in this life, and neither good nor evil can occur from this, rather, it is to be used as a tool to accomplish good. Thus, one must acknowledge that money cannot solve all problems as it does not come with instructions. Also, it cannot buy happiness, and can consume a lot of time, distracting us from our relationship with God, breeding greed. Thus, one needs to develop a biblical financial plan and commitment to apply, for it will provide guidance that will lift from the burden of being out of control financially and in life.

The Views on Giving

Society says that it is better to receive than to give. For many years, corporate America has prided itself on providing a high dividend for investors; they are always looking to stay competitive and provide high earnings on their reports. So, they minimize costs through corporate restructuring and cutting operations. But, through the social awareness trends, corporate America participates with different nonprofit organizations to start giving back to the community. Even before the government social programs or corporate programs, the church was at the forefront of ministering to the poor and needy, as Jesus commanded the church to do so in His name. Thus, the church must be light regarding giving and support in Jesus' name.

The scripture mentions a lot about giving, with more verses related to giving than any other subject on money. There are many instructions and examples concerning stewardship that promote generosity and giving. The attitude matters when one gives; 1 Corinthians 13:3[279], when fed the poor without love, it profits nothing. Thus, giving should be motivated by love, and should be personal, periodic, and premeditated.

Giving has benefits, such as increased intimacy, and can also create a relationship where there is a healthy balance of one

---

[279] 1 Corinthians 13:3

receiving and giving. The Scriptures illustrate that giving one's own things is evidence of God's grace in a person's life, developing the character and using God's gift to fulfill the purpose of His will. God is raising His people to be like Him, giving. When one gives to serve God, one is building and investing in the future kingdom of God. One should give to family, the local church, Christian ministers, and the poor with prayer, provision, and recognition of what Jesus has done and asked one to do. It is more of a blessing to give than receive, as Jesus said to all. Acts 20:35[280], one should not forget that giving is so significant to God because giving is a way to give of yourself.

The Tithe

To tithe is to give a portion of the whole, ten percent, from the secular historical records and perspective for a religious purpose. After the Noahic flood, there was money and property to support a religious purpose near Mesopotamia, Syria, Palestine, Greece, and as far west as the Phoenician city of Cartage. There were cases where civil taxation diverted to religious usage as well. Thus, it is known to practice tithing widely around Abram's surroundings in a pagan culture.

Abraham recognized Melchizedek as a high priest[281] and a genuine representation of God, YHWH, Jehovah, "I am who I am"[282] to offer the tithe. The blessing given by Melchizedek led Abram to give God a religious offering through Melchizedek. The tithe collection is uniquely priestly; the tithe was paid to a higher priest by a lower priest. Abram clearly stated that he owed allegiance to no other god or person except his personal God. In

---

[280] Acts 20:35

[281] Genesis 14:18-20

[282] Exodus 3:14-15

the Mosaic times, Tithes as follows, First Tithe, Levites Tithe, Festival Tithe, and Poor Tithe, all required specific giving of what would be given as a tithe, both giver and receiver. One says that giving is not based on tithing, and one says tithing is not giving.

Many in Christian circles propose that offering is giving; it states that the Old Testament tithe is not a model or pattern; one gives in proportion to his abundance because, in that abundance, God has supplied enough for one's self and others. Thus, Christians must support ministry, ordained by Christ and led by the Holy Spirit, not just through the tithe but with all means to support. Also, the New Testament giving does not set a rule for giving nor an exact amount to give, but it is based on the principle on the heart of giving. According to abundance, these principles make giving limitless, and we must trust God's providence to give accordingly, while being led by the Holy Spirit.

The way in which the New Testament church and Israel gave were vastly different. Israel was a national entity with defined borders, a national government, a national religion, and a theocracy. The people of Israel farmed the land of Israel. Their tithes came from their land to benefit their nation. On the other hand, the New Testament church is a collection of those individuals united to Christ throughout the world, an expatriate of heaven, and a foreigner living in a foreign land. The New Testament church believes that God provides all possessions one has as a tool to live in this world and is used as support in spreading the gospel. So, the New Testament challenges the Old Testament's mandatory giving. Christ challenges every believer to dedicate one hundred percent of his (or her) person and possessions to his service and use it to fulfill God's purpose through participation. We should not let ourselves become legalistic by just participating in giving tithe, implying that nothing more than a tithe is required and can lead to one not accepting

Christ's calling to give more.

On the other hand, many also follow the principle of the tithing model; 10% directly contribute to the local church, fulfilling the judicial requirement. They make a clear distinction between giving and tithe. The offering of giving is voluntary contributions above the tithe, which can go to any ministry or directly to the poor. The tithe shows the importance of obedient faith, acknowledging who God is and everything that belongs to Him. God expects His people to be obedient and give cheerfully with gratitude, and for that He will honor one's obedient faith.

The Biblical Stewardship

Faithfully living by God's biblical stewardship does not mean having a pile of money in the bank and less stress, but it means that complete trust is on His biblical principle. When one lives with faith and applies the biblical principle of stewardship, one will recognize that God controls all circumstances, provides all our needs, and has a clear conscience before God and others. With God in control, there should be nothing to fear but excitement for what He has planned. Many declare themselves financially free; but one should speak this declaration with caution. Because God is the provider of all our needs, we need to know He is the one who brings peace and contentment, not any achievements of works.

The Lord created all things and never transferred His creation's ownership. He blessed the creation and entrusted humanity to be a good steward of His creation. Thus, God holds all things together by His power. One needs to transfer the ownership of all things to God, for He is the rightful owner of all creation. Many say that God owns it all, but they still desperately hold on to all their possessions.

The one practical application is to establish the habit of

acknowledging God's ownership every time one spends or gives money; it will lessen the temptation of discontentment. God controls all things, and He will accomplish His will to develop one's character and integrity while also disciplining one to mature into greater faith. God will predictably and unpredictably provide all needs, making us realize that being faithful in all His gifts is to develop one's gratitude toward Him. He teaches all to give regularly and generously, tithe is the standard to follow but be open as God may prompt you to give more, and when this time comes we must be ready to be obedient and fulfill God's will.

God calls us to absolute honesty because the society that we live in asks us to live a compromised life that brings dishonesty to God. Honest behavior or action is an issue of faith, especially when we are called to be good stewards. A direct, honest action might look foolish in light of the circumstances, but every honest action will strengthen one's faith in the living God. When living dishonestly it leads to mistrust. We need to know that dishonesty permanently injures people. We need to know that even a small act of dishonesty is devastating; furthermore, it will lead to a broken relationship with God and others. In the process, dishonesty will destroy everything we build up. We need to know that God is the God of truth. Thus, we need to seek what is truth and seek holiness, for He is holy.[283]

Setting priorities is essential in being a good steward; first, one needs to develop a closer relationship with Jesus Christ. One also needs to teach the word of God and share the love of God through proclaiming Jesus to all. God called all those following him to do good work in the field where He has placed them. He called not to stop but to use the gift of talents and develop the gifts to use it for His glory. The practical aspect of financial responsibility is

---

[283] 1 Peter 1:15-16

living within one's means, just as taught in Proverbs[284], is to work hard not to be lazy, not to overindulge in spending, but spend wisely and save for the rainy days like the ants, determine the wants and needs, live in contentment.[285] God will direct and guide one's steps to live a balanced life defined by His will in one's life as one allows Him to.

Now, on the practical side of living with a budget, a plan for spending money wisely provides an opportunity to pray about spending decisions and putting trust in God's providence. When one creates a budget, it recognizes where things are at the moment; it reveals the areas that are not in good standing. Without a budget, one cannot help but be overwhelmed by everything. Thus, creating a perfect map of where one starts and needs to go is key to successfully getting there as planned, with help from God's guidance, of course. The key to solid budgeting is adding to income and reducing expenses, categorizing and sorting based on needs and wants, tithing, giving, and future savings.

Knowing how everyone walks on this journey is one key principle that will lighten the burden of keeping the budget. Many believers who trust God are on a journey as a pilgrim; thus, they learn to acquire only those possessions that enable them to fulfill God's calling. The second key is to make an effort to live simply; maintaining every possession requires time, attention, and money. The best thing we can do to grow in our relationship with the Lord is to spend time with Him. This time spent with Him will help us to truly understand His love for us. The third key is to recognize that the enemy of God has proclaimed war. Christ called us to fight against anything hindering our faith in Him and to not conform to this world. The fourth key is to spend wisely, please God, and not

---

[284] Proverbs 6:6-11

[285] Hebrews 13:5

compare our worth with what others may have; rather we must focus on the things that matter most in our lives, and continually love others.

God is involved in everything, especially when we are called His steward. First, God loves us whether we have been good stewards or not. He loves us as we put our trust in Him and know that God is in control and has a purpose for all good and bad things. Thus, we are called to trust in Him continually. Faith in God is important in every aspect of our lives, especially when dealing with being a good steward, whether that is when ministering to an individual or a community of believers.

Group Discussion

Leaders: Explain the importance of knowing who we are to God as good stewards. First, share your thoughts about being a good steward and how God provided your needs and how you manage finances. Then, review the questions and answers by finding the reference bible verses and reference pages in the book.

1. What did God instruct Adam and Eve to do? Genesis 1:28

2. How did He create mankind? Genesis 1:27

3. What is the root of all kinds of evil? 1 Timothy 6:10

4. What does it mean to serve God? Is God fair to all doing His work? Is He fair to you? Matthew 20:1-16

5. What does the parable of talent teach us? Matthew 25:14-30

6. What does God want us to do? Deuteronomy 6:5

7. What does the seeking of wealth eventually lead to? Ecclesiastes 5:10

8. Can one serve God and mammon? Luke 16:13

9. Why did Jesus mention that it is hard for a rich man to enter the kingdom of God? Matthew 19:23

10. How are we supposed to give when we feed the poor? 1 Corinthians 13:3

11. Who did Abraham recognize as a high priest? Genesis 14:18-20

12. Who is YHWH? Exodus 3:14-15

13. What does God want us to do as a good steward? Proverbs 6:6-11

14. Where should we focus on this world or the Kingdom of God? Matthew 6:19

15. What do we need to do to overcome the covetousness? Hebrews 13:5

16. Why is giving is important? Acts 20:35

17. Please share your experience with money.

18. Did you run into financial troubles? If you did, how did it happen, and how did you overcome it? Luke 12:15-34, Matthew 6:25-34

19. What is your definition of success? Luke 10:20, Luke 9:48, Mark 9:35

20. What does it mean to you to be a good steward? 1 Cor. 15:10

CHAPTER 7
STEP 7, LIVING AS A DISCIPLE/WITNESS

Who is a disciple?

We know how important it is to live in God's presence and follow his word. But is this all that God asked us to live by? There is more to being a disciple than just having a relationship with God alone. We would be no different from monks in the early church, who were so out of touch with the world that they could not truly live out in faith or be obedient to God's word completely. Martin Luther had firsthand experience of how hard it is to live out in faith, being isolated from society, dedicating his life to the monastery without interacting with others, and spreading God's word to the people, the truth that lives within the power of God. Thus, we must live out the faith in God's Grace that transforms us and others.

We know that God is love. He demonstrated his love through Christ, and renewed us through the work of the Holy Spirit; for these reasons, we live in God's eternal provision of his perfect will. But Jesus gave us a very important last word that we must remember and act upon. Matthew 28:19–20, Jesus speaking to the disciples, "Go therefore and make disciples of all the nations, baptizing them in the name of the Father and of the Son and of the Holy Spirit, teaching them to observe all things that I have commanded you; and lo, I am with you always, even to the end of the age." [286]

"Therefore" means that in all we know and have experienced through Christ, there can be no other truth but the truth that exists within Jesus Christ, whom they were disciples to be ready for, through seeing many miracles, teachings, and also the death and resurrection. The disciples are instructed to act upon, based on, all that Jesus Christ has taught them and experienced in their lives. Jesus instructs them to go and make disciples of all nations. Jesus breaks down all the barriers that might exist in a society that discriminates against others based on culture and class. The first thing to happen in the relationship is to connect with mutual trust. God initiated the connection; thus, we are all connected, and our broken relationship is mended through Christ. He has made us new; now, we are his followers and disciples, just like the Apostolic disciples. There are no distinctions here; there might be time differences, such as seeing Jesus Christ in person and being witnesses, but we are instructed very much the same as the original disciples. This does not diminish the original twelve chosen apostles; they have been the first to everything in a unique way where they have been used mightily for the kingdom of God and establishing the church, as they lay down their lives for spreading the good news.

We are to connect with people, which means that we need to be relational with people; our goal is to share the good news of

---

[286] New King James Version

Jesus Christ, but first of all, we need to be genuine with others. Thus, we should teach them God's word, whether they know God or are just beginning to know God and his Word and lead them patiently. But, there is importance in how we need to disciple others. We must do it in the name of the Father, Son, and the Holy Spirit. Why is this so important to us? Through earlier chapters in the book, God the Father, God the Son, and God the Holy Spirit are distinct persons with one essence; we focus on how important it is to accept this truth as the foundation. If this truth deviates in any way, then there cannot be the truth. Because Scripture is unambiguous with whom God is, and the Tribune God exists within the Scripture. Without God's sovereign plan, Christ's crucifixion and resurrection, or the work of the Holy Spirit, lives cannot be transformed through the accepting of Christ. But through Him, we could see the perfect will of God complete through the Father, Son, and Holy Spirit working together.

Meanwhile, we are to teach the perfect will of God and all that is written in God's word. We cannot ignore the truth in the scripture, but the world wants to distort and destroy God's word from people's lives, especially believers, to stay in infant mode. Satan is doing an excellent job of making Christians stay sterile and become ineffective in doing God's work. Thus, we need to learn first of God's word and live accordingly, and then, we must truly teach. As we do, God will be with us and use us to make a difference in the lives of others. Yes, our lives will be filled with God's peace and blessing.

A disciple, in Greek literal translation, means "student." So, we need to become a student of Christ. We are to learn from His teaching and His word. Many Christians, when asked to be a disciple of Christ, put too much emphasis on the commitment that comes with being called a disciple. Yes, there is a definite commitment to being called a disciple, as discipleship requires a committed life mentioned in Luke 14:33: "So likewise, whoever of you does not forsake all that he has cannot be My disciple." [287] Sacrifice is expected: Jesus said to his disciples in Matthew 16:24, "If anyone would come after me, he must deny himself and take up his cross and follow me."[288] The committed life is not a short term volunteer kind of thing to feel good; instead it requires a true sacrifice of giving and serving, not for short term, rather up to where God's purpose is fulfilled.

But, as you accept Christ into your heart, you are called to follow Jesus Christ, which carries a commitment to leaving your past life behind to serve him. As a follower of Jesus Christ, you belong to Christ. You are being transformed into the likeness of Christ.[289] We are all called to be disciples and commanded by Christ to share His good news with all who need to be heard. But, many do not want to be called a disciple or commit to proclaiming the good news of Jesus Christ because many only want to sacrifice what they are willing to.

Let's understand how people know of "disciple," old and new. When Jesus called the original disciples, rather than choosing those of high class with an exceptional educational background, he did quite the opposite. He selected those who did not have these backgrounds. He chose the ordinary man to show he would work through them mightily. Let's start with Peter, who is also called Simon, used to be a fisherman[290], well known to be one that was close to Jesus, later called a pillar of the church.[291] But, his

---

[287] New King James Version

[288] New King James Version

[289] 2 Corinthians 3:18

[290] Luke 5:10

[291] Galatians 2:9

personality and attitude, shows his imperfectness, passionate yet strong-willed self, who is impulsive and rushes into his emotion. Yet, Christ shows and teaches him to become the leader among the disciples and also becomes one whom God used to build the church after the ascension of Christ. Jesus taught Peter with patience to not be afraid, and to be faithful.[292] As we can see, Peter was no saint or one who was worthy to be called to be a disciple or apostle. Still, through Christ's patience and love for Peter, he became a faithful apostle who sacrificed all for God, and endured until the end. We need to know that when one is called, it is truly a gift from God, and we cannot allow our weakness to stop us from serving God, learning from God, or not trusting him. Rather, we need to trust and follow his ways.

We cannot forget John, who was called to serve Christ, who spoke the word of God mightily, and received the vision of what would come at the Island of Patmos in his last days. John was in the inner circle of Christ like Peter, but in the early days, he acted aggressively and recklessly. With the teaching of Christ in his life, he brought transformation and maturity and became passionate and zeal-filled with spreading the good news he had received. Originally, John was filled with a strong zeal for Christ to become a king, like other disciples, wanting to be in a prominent position. But Christ changed him through his teaching, redirected his passion with humbleness, and proclaimed the truth with the love of Jesus Christ.

On the other hand, we know of Judas Iscariot, who betrayed Christ and committed suicide. What was the difference that existed among other disciples who died for Christ? Judas was focused not on Christ but on what he would bring to him. Judas thought of money, driven by the power that will come through

---

[292] Psalm 32:8

Christ, which overruled everything Christ had taught him over three years of ministry that he was involved in and experienced. Many within the church today go to church but are not truly saved. Because they never truly accepted Christ in their heart, they were attracted to what Christ has to offer for them and other things that come within, belonging to the Church as churchgoers. We could fall into this same gradual, subtle temptation when we do not look to Christ and who he is to us. When we are called to be a disciple of Christ, we are called to give up all our things.[293] Of course, we are saved by the grace of God, not like Judas, who never accepted Christ, but we cannot ignore the truth that we will also get tempted; thus, we need to put our eyes on Jesus.

Paul was not an original apostle of twelve, but Christ called him to follow him as a disciple while he went to Damascus to persecute the church. He was a Pharisee, knowledgeable, a bit rigid, very educated, and passionate about God and his law being kept before his encounter with Jesus. But, His encounter with Jesus changed his life completely; as he found the truth that he did not know and eventually used his knowledge for Christ. He was transformed and would go on to continually spread the goodness of Jesus Christ on his journey to many different cities in Greece. We were sinners, but God forgave us our sins. We could be used, like Paul, to make a difference in God's kingdom.

Now, who are you closer in touch with between Peter, Judas, John, and Paul? There is no right or wrong answer. Remember, no one is perfect to follow, but God uses those who are willing and not always ready. There should be a distinction made by those who proclaim to be a disciple or witness for Christ. We will never be prepared to be faithful disciples or witnesses to this world. But, through the Grace of God, we are always ready and

---

[293] Luke 14:33

willing when we are not equipped.

Knowing Oneself

Many who proclaim to be Christian genuinely know God, but without taking the necessary first steps of accepting God's grace in their heart through what Jesus Christ did on the cross, they are no different than Judas Iscariot, who betrayed Christ at the most critical moment. But God turns the betrayal of Judas for silver[294] into fulfilling His will. We cannot allow the unrighteousness of those who do not believe[295] to influence our faith. Through faith in Jesus Christ, we are God's children[296] and know and understand that we no longer belong to this world but belong to God and are sanctified. Thus, we must always examine our hearts and actions living as a disciple or witness.

In today's society, it is so easy to get swayed by self-deception for this is normal, of seeking comfortable or easy lives as long as one does not harm others, everything is good. We can witness this now more, with technical advancements where manual work has transformed robotic, and continually advancing where more is completed with less. Even within our lifestyle, we want to take the easy route, not the hard path that requires tedious work. This is not all bad, but when one falls into the way of moral decay, or are unethical, in their actions toward others, there is bound to be a deception that leads to destruction, whether spiritual or just reality of events. Thus, we need to live in truth and speak the truth, and also not deceive ourselves.[297] We need to know that we cannot

---

[294] Matthew 26:14-16

[295] Matthew 21:32

[296] John 1:12

[297] 1 John 1:8

trust our hearts since we do not always know our hearts.[298] Therefore, we need God's word to work and guide us in our hearts. If we are not living like Christ and live a compromised life, then there cannot be truth in the life that we are living. If we live our lives in unrighteousness, then we are to purify through the blood of Jesus.[299] Hence, we need to rely on the Holy Spirit[300] to lead and transform us into faithful witnesses that follow the image of Christ.[301] To know that we are in Christ truly, we must examine ourselves through the word of God[302] and not look to others for validation. Paul exhorts in his letter that all believers are athletes racing to the finish line.[303] Thus, we are ready to do God's work by recognizing ourselves before the Lord and impacting the world with God's word. But, we need not be too focused on ourselves, with self-help, self-love, and self-worth, which the world uses to promote philosophical solutions and cultural norms to make one only trust oneself.

Many seek to improve their low self-esteem by reaching the many available options on self-help, hoping to improve their self-image. But, low self-esteem itself is also a form of pride. They seek attention from others for their situation and where they focus on it. Some receive the help they seek from those self-help books, but most turn back to their old ways. But we are different or need to be different from those seeking self-value or worth. As we know, we are created in God's image and his children. Thus, we belong with one another as believers; we are not to consider

---

[298] Jeremiah 17:9

[299] 1 John 1:7

[300] 1 Corinthians 2:10

[301] Romans 8:20

[302] Galatians 6:4

[303] 1 Corinthians 9:24

ourselves worth more[304] or less, but we must know that we stand before God for his grace and mercy.

Knowing God's will

Many seek God's will and wonder what God's will is. We are always to pray to God for direction and our will. Thus, we will be filled with the Holy Spirit, who gives us wisdom and understanding.[305] Hence, we cannot rush into doing something that we will regret, thinking that it was the will of God; rather, we must seek out with patience, constantly testing[306] and examining the will of God.

The utmost important principle we need to apply to know the will of God is to give thanks in all circumstances[307], for if we do not, we would not be doing it for God with a heart of love. Instead, it will be more of obligation or responsibility, where there is no joy. First, we need to be separated, for we are not following the world; we are to do what is good and perfect in what God is leading us to do by transforming our minds[308] to think of his will in our lives. Thus, we will be a witness to those who are ignorant and silence them by doing what is good.[309] We will let them see their foolishness so they will know that their foolishness is blinding them and lead them to understand what God wants them to see, by sharing the word of God. Also, we must be patient and endure, for God will deliver what he has promised[310] when we share the good

---

[304] Romans 12:3

[305] Colossians 4:12

[306] Romans 12:2

[307] 1 Thessalonians 5:18

[308] Romans 12:2

[309] 1 Peter 2:15

[310] Hebrews 10:36

news of Jesus Christ. When one knows the will of God, there can be only God's will for one[311], not the desires that will pass by like the world. Thus, one should suffer for doing what is good.[312] We need to know that suffering is good for us when we are doing God's will, for God will deliver his good plan and fulfill his plan through us. We are not alone when we follow God's will; we are all connected and related by the bond of his will. So, one who does the will of God could be brother and sister[313] in Christ even though they do not know each other. God will supply all our needs according to his plan and riches in Christ Jesus.[314]

Knowing the Warnings sign of times

In today's society, it is important to be awake and share the good news of Jesus Christ with this world because the urgency is there, and we must also be aware of the changes occurring in our culture and world. There are warning signs of how the world is becoming more corrupt and destructive as a society. When we look at human history, destruction, and war are just part of history. It is a repeated cycle that will continue continually, one might profess. What does it matter if it's just a cycle that will repeat? Yes, it may be on the surface, but the frequency of increased disasters and the immorality of humanity will be the ultimate warning signs for us as believers.

Knowing the Prophecy

When we look at the book of Revelation, God gives us more detail about what will happen in the end times and how Jesus Christ will come back to fulfill the last prophecy. First, the warning signs that

---

[311] 1 John 2:17

[312] 1 Peter 3:17

[313] Mark 3:35

[314] Philippians 4:19

somewhat align with the time that we are living in but not at the extreme are mentioned in Luke 21:11, "And there will be great earthquakes in various places, and famines and pestilences, and there will be fearful sights and great signs from heaven."[315] Secondly, more will tune their ears to false teachings and false teachers to fill their spiritual needs. Thirdly, there will also be revivals and disciplining with the gospel by the leading of the Holy Spirit. Thus, it will be very relevant to who belongs to God and who is not.

Revelation to the Churches

John, as he wrote the Book of Revelation, starts with writing letters to the seven churches to encourage and reveal what is to come; meanwhile, this also applies to the church today. The Seven Letters to the church start with grace and peace from the tribune God and John to the churches, letting the church know that the Lord, who is coming, sets the revelation of what is to come. The encounter with Christ and the commission he receives to see and explain the mystery explain that the lamp stands represent seven churches. The letter to Ephesus asks the church to return to their first love for the Lord, for they have forgotten.[316] The letter to Smyrna says to stay faithful and not be afraid of death, stay strong to suffering and persecution continually.[317] The letter to Pergamos asks the church to repent and not fall into false doctrine and influences of the time.[318] The letter to Thyatira asks churches

---

[315] New King James Version

[316] Revelation 2:1-7

[317] Revelation 2:8-11

[318] Revelation 2:12-17

not to fall into a false prophetess and not compromise.[319] The letter to Sardis asks the church not to be spiritually dead and not to fall asleep.[320] The letter to Philadelphia asks the church to keep the faith, keep his name, and endure patiently.[321] The letter to Laodicea asks the church not to be lukewarm in their faith and not to be content with living a compromised life of wealth and idolatry.[322] The importance of the letter to seven churches, in recognition of their condition and needs, John addressed accordingly, encouraging the church to keep their faith. We need to know ourselves and our condition and seek to keep our faith in times to come.

The Role of Seven-Sealed Scrolls

John explains the seven-sealed scrolls and how the seals will reveal God's plan. John saw the Throne[323], the twenty-four elders[324], the four living creatures[325], and the sealed scroll with seven seals.[326] John is searching for one to break the seals, one worthy of judgment over evil and judging the world. John saw the lamb's appearance and witnessed the lamb's worship; angels and creation joined the song to praise him as the seal was being broken. As each seal is broken, a new judgment is unleashed on the earth through

---

[319] Revelation 2:18-29

[320] Revelation 3:1-6

[321] Revelation 3:7-13

[322] Revelation 3:14-22

[323] Revelation 4:1-3

[324] Revelation 4:4-5

[325] Revelation 4:6-11

[326] Revelation 5:1-4

one who is instructed to.

The first seal opened and saw the horseman on a white horse to conquer; some believe one is Christ, and most say one is an Antichrist coming as one will provide peace to the world.[327] As the second seal opened, the horseman on a red horse with a great sword started the war, the worst of the war seen on the earth.[328] The third seal opened and saw the third horseman with a black horse, bringing the famine and hard life with little to survive.[329] The fourth seal opened and saw the horseman with the power to kill the fourth of the world's population through war, famine, and wild animals.[330] The fifth seal opened and witnessed those whom saints had slain for the word of God, asking justice for those martyred for God.[331] The sixth seal opened and witnessed catastrophic natural disasters such as earthquakes that affected the earth's sun, moon, and atmosphere, causing the people to hide in caves.[332] God's servants instructed the sealing; the one hundred and forty-four thousand were sealed and innumerable.[333] Once the seventh seal opened, there was silence in heaven for about half an hour, a prelude to worse judgments.[334]

The Seven Trumpets of Judgment

John writes about the seven trumpets, the contents of the seventh

---

[327] Revelation 6:1-2

[328] Revelation 6:3-4

[329] Revelation 6:5-6

[330] Revelation 6:7-8

[331] Revelation 6:9-11

[332] Revelation 6:12-17

[333] Revelation 7:1-17

[334] Revelation 8:1

seal judgment, which occurs during the Great Tribulation period. The first trumpet sounded, and hail and fire with blood burned one-third of trees and grass, consumed in ashes, the symbol of God's judgment upon the earth and causing an imbalance in the ecosystem.[335] The second trumpet sounded, a massive fireball like a meteorite hit, and a third of the sea became blood; death was followed by a third of sea creatures and the destruction of ships.[336] The third trumpet sounded, and a great star fell; a burning torch brought the death of a third of fresh waters and caused many men's deaths.[337] The fourth trumpet sounded, bringing the darkness where a third of the sun, moon, and stars were struck, which brought changes in heaven. There was a warning of the woes of those on the earth after the fourth trumpet.[338] The fifth trumpet sounded; the demonic locust, allowed to torture, not to kill, was released to cause pain to unsaved men for five months; these men did not have the seal of God on their foreheads. The identity of the locust varies with a different interpretation: an army of Satan or creatures or warriors.[339] The sixth trumpet sounded, and the second woe came under the work of four wicked angels to prepare two hundred million horsemen to kill a third of humanity.[340] Before the seventh trumpet sounded, John witnessed angels appearing and told John to prophesy some more. Then came the two witnesses prophesied for 1260 days, clothed in sackcloth, preached in Jerusalem and performed a miracle, murdered and raised them

---

[335] Revelation 8:7

[336] Revelation 8:8-9

[337] Revelation 8:10-11

[338] Revelation 8:12-13

[339] Revelation 9:1-12

[340] Revelation 9:13-21

back to life, taking them to heaven.[341] The seventh trumpet sounded, the temple of God in heaven opened, an ark of the covenant could be seen, lightning, noises, thunder, earthquakes, and great hail.[342]

John mentions seven performers during the great tribulations: the woman who symbolizes Israel[343], the red dragon which is Satan[344], the child of the woman who symbolizes Jesus Christ[345], Michael, the archangel, wars with the dragon[346], the dragon persecutes the woman[347], Remnant of Israel[348], the wild beast out of the sea, a political power and a person[349] where the wild beast defies God and takes control of people to be worshiped by it.[350] Also, another wild beast out of the earth who is a religious leader, assumes the role of authority, deceives and delusions the world, asks people to receive the sign of beast, 666.[351] Thus, it leads to the end of the great tribulation, those who stand with faith[352], the continual proclaiming of the gospel[353], and praise those who die

---

[341] Revelation 10:11-14

[342] Revelation 11:15-19

[343] Revelation 12:1-2

[344] Revelation 12:3-4

[345] Revelation 12:5-6

[346] Revelation 12:7-12

[347] Revelation 12:13-16

[348] Revelation 12:17

[349] Revelation 13:1-10

[350] Revelation 13:11-18

[351] Revelation 13:11-18

[352] Revelation 14:1-5

[353] Revelation 14:6-7

in the Lord[354], but judgment declared on Babylon and those with the mark of the beat[355] Thus, the final preparation mentioned in Revelation 15 and pouring out of seven bowls of wrath in Revelation 16, is ready to bring forth the final judgments on the earth.

The Seven Last Plagues to Come

The final judgments of the tribulation period, the most severe judgments the world has ever seen, are of another name, "the seven bowls of God's wrath." The first plague, shown as the first bowl, pours out and will cause painful sores upon those who worshiped Antichrist with the mark of the beast[356]; the saints will not be affected.

The second plague, the second bowl poured out, turning the sea into blood, so all that had life would die. The death of saltwater marine life will destroy a significant food source for millions of people. The second trumpet had already killed one-third of sea life; with this plague, the rest of sea life had perished, and the ocean was officially dead.[357]

The third plague came after the pour out of the third bowl; the freshwater will become blood. This plague will destroy freshwater fish, further impacting people's food supply.[358]

The fourth plague, the fourth bowl, will cause the sun to become dangerously hot as "to scorch men with fire." There was

---

[354] Revelation 14:13

[355] Revelation 14:8-12

[356] Revelation 16:2

[357] Revelation 16:3

[358] Revelation 16:4-7

no repentance, they cursed the name of God, they refused to give glory to God, and their genuine wickedness is demonstrated very strongly.[359]

The fifth plague, the fifth bowl, punishment will bring darkness, pains, and sores to the beast's kingdom. Some live in agony, intensified by their pain and suffering, but they are still not repented.[360]

The sixth plague, the sixth bowl, containing this plague, will be poured out on the Euphrates River, drying up and making land travel easier for the armies of the whole world to assemble at Armageddon. From this location, the assembled armies will advance toward Jerusalem for a final battle against Jesus Christ on the Day of the Lord.[361]

In Revelation 16:17, Seventh plague, the final bowl of wrath, a loud voice from heaven, said: "It is done."[362] The final wrath consists of noises, thundering, lightning, and such a mighty and great earthquake as had not occurred since men were on the earth." Jerusalem is split into three parts, and the cities of the world collapse. Islands are flooded, and mountains disappear. God uses this to represent the seven last punishments that He will pour out on sinful humanity.[363]

The Great Babylon Falls, Marriage Supper of the Lamb, the Judgment, and the Millennium

---

[359] Revelation 16:8-9

[360] Revelation 16:10-11

[361] Revelation 16:12

[362] New King James Version

[363] Revelation 16:17-21

The great Harlot, who sits on a scarlet Beast and by many waters known as Babylon the Great, rules over the earth's kings, influences all people, promotes religious heresy, and leads people into corruption. The angel showing John the vision of the Harlot and the scarlet Beast reveals their identities and fates and wages war against Jesus Christ. Christ destroys New Babylon. Then, the people of the Earth, such as the kings, merchants, and sailors, mourn the permanence of New Babylon's destruction.[364]

    A great multitude praises God for destroying the great harlot. The Marriage Supper of the Lamb depicts the wedding feast of the Lamb, Jesus, and His bride, the Church. The Christ on a white horse brings forth the Judgment of the two Beasts, the Dragon and the Dead. Thus, the Beast and the False Prophet are cast into the Lake of Fire. The Dragon, Satan, has been imprisoned in the Bottomless Pit for a thousand years. The resurrected saints live and reign with Christ for a thousand years. After the Thousand Years, Satan is released and deceives the nations in the four corners of the Earth, Gog and Magog, and gathers them for battle at the holy city. They made war against the people of God but faced defeat.[365] The Dragon is cast into the Lake of Fire with the Beast and the False Prophet. At the Last Judgment, the great white throne judgment: the wicked, along with Death and Hades, are cast into the Lake of Fire, the second death.[366]

The New Earth and New Heaven

All things are made new. It is the dwelling place of believers in Christ. The New Heaven, Earth, and New Jerusalem replace Old Heaven and Old Earth. There is no more suffering or death. God

---

[364] Revelation 17-18

[365] Revelation 19

[366] Revelation 20

comes to dwell with humanity in the New Jerusalem, and the glory of the New Jerusalem is demonstrated. The River of Life and the Tree of Life appear, healing the nations and peoples. The curse of sin is no more; no death, no mourning, no weeping, no pain, no more curse, no more night. Jesus testifies to the Churches that he is coming soon and does his commandants; blessed are those who do his commands and warn those not to add or edit things shown.[367]

What to come and what to believe?

We wait on the Lord for his return. For he has promised his return to his disciples in his ascension, he will return just as his ascension and according to the revelations that were shared with John in the book of Revelation. Meanwhile, Jesus proclaimed and commanded; he instructed the disciples to spread the good news to all who needed to hear. We must act on this by being a faithful witness to this world. But, we need to know what we believe in the coming of the Lord, as shared in the book of Revelation. Thus, studying eschatology plays a key role, where it is the study of future things through scripture. The four main views, premillennialism, dispensationalism, postmillennialism, and amillennialism, strongly support notable conservative giants of faith. The common theme of the return of Christ overrules the interpretation based on each millennium view proponent's different approaches.

Premillennialism believes that the second coming of Christ will proceed to the millennial kingdom. Thus, the world will get worse; Christ will return. Premillennialists believe it is best to approach literally in Revelation 20, believing in one thousand years of Christ's reign after his return, with his saints here on earth before the installation of the eternal new heavens and new earth. The Millennium reign will have peace and justice through enforcing

---

[367] Revelation 21-22

the rule of Christ over all, saved or unsaved. Then, at the end of his reign, Satan releases and puts humanity to one final test before the final judgment. This natural reading of Revelation 20:1-6 is based on doctrine. [368]The principle is based on applying the literal system of biblical interpretation. The Bible is a source in which truth is collected, compared, and placed in their logical relations into systematic theology; put, "take God at His Word." The focus is set on aligning and consistent with its New Testament context and its Christology.

Dispensationalists believe in the centrality of national Israel in God's plan and rapture of Christians to heaven before the beginning of the Tribulation. Thus, dispensationalism takes the principle of taking the scriptures in their literal and normal sense, an understanding that applies to the entire Bible. Meanwhile, the literal approach to teaching the kingdom's premillennial dispensation doctrine is basic.

Premillennialism points to the fact that God is progressively moving through history and directing the course of events to a good end, righteous ending with justice and setting up the kingdom. Dispensationalism is double "pre-s," Pre-tribulation Pre-millennialists added distinct tents regarding the Church and the Jews and fulfillment of Old Testament prophecies, which is led by the literal interpretation of Scripture, a clear distinction between Israel and the church.

Postmillennialism is that preaching the gospel and the saving work of the Holy Spirit will eventually Christianize the world, as of the last things which hold that the kingdom of God is now in the present and coming days till the final return of Christ. Also, the Kingdom of God is the product of the works of the Holy

---

[368] New King James Version

Spirit connected with sharing the gospel. Thus, postmillennialists believe in not too many changes but relatively gradual conformity to Christianity and also place a strong focus on the universal of Christ's work of redemption, along with the emphasis on reform through law and the Gospel, the political and cultural spheres inclined toward the pretest approach to Revelation. Postmillennialist believe the world will turn for the better to God and that preaching the gospel will see most of the world converted, thus bringing an earthly millennium before the second coming.

    Amillennialism has the tradition; of church fathers such as Origen and Augustine, old as the Church itself, which is not from modern theologians. Amillenarians reject a literal, earthly, materialistic millennium like the premillennialists. The Amillenarians believe there will be no millennium. Amillenarians believe pre- and post-millenarians are hyper-literal interpretations of obscure passages of Scripture. There can be no literalists because they can also spiritualize many Scripture passages. Amillenarians believe God has one eternal plan of Salvation. Old Testament saints were saved by looking for the cross of Christ. Amillenarians believe in two aspects of the one true church, the visible and invisible; all promises to national Israel have been fulfilled or invalidated through unbelief.

    The basis of Amillenarian's millennial doctrine is from two basic facts derived, the nature of the book of Revelation and the clear teaching of other scriptures relating to the subject matter of Revelation 20. [369] Also, progressive parallelism has seven sections that run parallel and depict the church and the word from when Christ's first comes to the second. The kingdom of God is central in human history, and Jesus Christ is the Lord of history. Thus, all of history is moving toward a goal; the redemption of the universe.

---

[369] New King James Version

So, the covenant of grace is still in effect today and will culminate in the eternal dwelling together of God and his redeemed people on the new earth.

Amillennialism, a thousand years as a symbolic number representing an indefinitely long time, the first coming of Christ until his second coming, as represented as the church age. The binding of Satan happened spiritually at the cross; the reigning of the saints is the present age; the loosing of Satan is a final period of deception, and the fire from heaven that devours the wicked is the second coming of Christ. The view of the last things holds that the Bible does not predict a millennium; instead, there will be a parallel between good and evil, God's kingdom, and Satan's kingdom in this world until the second coming of Christ. Amillennialism agrees with Premillennialism in teaching that a personal Antichrist appears shortly before the return of Christ. The tents of Amillennialism, like those of Premillennialism, allow its holders to be the main of the second coming.

The Three Views Rapture

Within the Christian worldview, the Rapture has a widespread word for great tribulation in Revelation, which believes that caught up in the air to meet the Lord. Based on 2 Thessalonians 2:1, John 14:3 and Matthew 25:1-3, one generation of believers is to be taken out of the world without dying.[370] Historic premillennialism holds that there is to be but one return of Christ, that is, one "second coming," which occurs immediately before the establishment of the millennial kingdom. However, modern dispensationalism holds that the Church is to go through the Tribulation; Matthew 24 mentions "a great tribulation,"[371] which comes forth post-

---

[370] New King James Version

[371] New King James Version

tribulation view, weakness on the clear teaching of those who have faith will never experience God's wrath. Also, based on Matthew 24 and Daniel 7:25[372], the mid-tribulation view believes that the church will face tribulation and catch up after three and a half years. The Mid-tribulation view fails on the same note where the clear teaching of those who have faith will never be God's wrath.[373]

Dispensationalist holds that the Rapture occurs before the Tribulation, with Christ in the air, who returns at the end of the seven-year and establishes the millennial kingdom. Also, 1 Thessalonians 4 states that the unsaved will not be resurrected when the saints are, along with Paul's statement in verse 16 that the dead in Christ shall rise first.[374] Dispensationalism thus sets for the second coming of Christ for his Saints, which they term the Rapture, and a visible coming of Christ seven years later with His saints, which they term the Revelations. There is a clear distinction between Israel and the church for dispensationalists, which will happen in the millennium. But A-millennialists believe the Church fulfills Israel's prophecies, being true spiritual Israel. Post and A-millennialists believe that the Rapture comes at the end of the present world order. However, postmillennialists believe that the Millennium precedes it. In contrast, Amillennialist believe there is no Millennium in the usual term, which relates to all Church age.

Where are we?

Knowing that Jesus Christ will come back soon, how the prophecies will be fulfilled, and what to watch for, we need to be awake and know the time is near. We must fulfill Jesus's greatest commandment spoken to disciples: sharing his good news

---

[372] New King James Version

[373] Romans 8:1

[374] New King James Version

throughout our lives. Correctly understanding the prophecies discussed here plays a significant role in not being deceived into following Satan instead of God. Many so-called Christian ministries try to make believers teach their ways and make them believe their way is the true way to serve God, with misleading teachings of the Word, especially the second coming of the Lord, through distortion and misinterpretation of the Word, use of God's Word to make one live with fear, thus, follow their teaching and ways. Many who talk of the coming of the Lord will use the Word of God to lead them on to trust in them and deceive many into a life that is filled with fear, where all talks of end times, where they cannot live Christ-filled lives or be a witness to the world by living with peace.

    The cults love to draw those keen on the Lord's coming and misdirect them to give off their lives for them. We cannot fall into this trap set by Satan and must also be prepared to help those lost in this trap out of the life of deception. We are to be faithful disciples by knowing what we are facing, what we are going against, and what will be waiting for us in the future. So, we will not be discouraged but encouraged to embrace God's plan in our lives, whether it is a storm or the sun shining down on us. We must continually take the step of faith and live as a true witness to this world by loving God more and loving others, as Christ has shown throughout his ministry and his teaching.

Group Discussion

Leaders: Explain the importance of knowing who we are to God as disciples and witnesses. First, share your thoughts about being a disciple and how God used you. Then, review the questions and answers by finding the reference bible verses and reference pages in the book.

1. What does it mean to be a disciple of Christ? Luke 14:33

2. Does following Christ require a sacrifice? Matthew 16:24

3. What did Jesus instruct the disciples to do when he was ascending? Matthew 28:19-20

4. What does it mean that we are transformed in the likeness of Christ? 2 Corinthians 3:18

5. Why did Peter call a pillar of the church? Galatians 2:9, Acts 2,

7 Steps to a Grace-Filled Life Right Now

Acts 8, Acts 10

6. Was Peter a perfect disciple? Luke 5:10, Matthew 14:28-29, Matthew 26:33

7. Who was Judas Iscariot? John 12:6

8. When we come to faith, we are called to give up what? Luke 14:33

9. Who was Paul? Philippians 3:5–6, Acts 9:1–22

10. Did God use Judas' betrayal? Matthew 26:14-16

11. Who must we rely on to lead and transform us? Romans 8:20, 1 Corinthians 2:10

12. How did Paul compare the believers? Galatians 6:4, 1 Corinthians 9:27

13. Who will provide our needs? Philippians 4:19

14. What will be the warning signs for the fulfillment of prophecy that John wrote in the book of revelation? Luke 21:11

15. What are the seven churches that John wrote to? Revelation 2-3

16. What did John write about to the Ephesus church? Revelation 2:1-7

17. What did John write about to the Smyrna church? Revelation 2:8-11

18. What did John write about to the Pergamos church? Revelation 2:12-17

19. What were the seven sealed scrolls? Revelation 6-7

20. What were the seven trumpets of judgment? Revelation 8-14

21. What were the seven last plagues to come? Revelation 16

22. What was the fall of the great Babylon? Revelation 17-18

23. When was the dragon cast in the lake of fire? Revelation 19-20

24. What does it mean that Christ will build a New Jerusalem? Revelation 21-22

25. What are the main views on what will happen in the second coming of the Lord? Explain your views.

26. What are three views on Rapture? Explain your views.

27. What do we need to do now?

28. How are we needed to finish the race? 2 Timothy 4:7

CONCLUSION

By understanding the Tribune God, God the Father, God the Son, God the Spirit, and those who stand against God, we are in a better place than before, where we will commune with God more deeply without any distractions or doubts. There can be only joy that will bring as God reminds us who he is to us. He is the heavenly father who loves us; thus, we must live like the children we are called to be. Hopefully, reading this book brought forth the knowledge and understanding of who God is to us. There can be only joy in knowing he is with us and watching over us. But God has entrusted us with being good stewards of all the good things God has given us, to take good care of. Meanwhile, being faithful means not only serving the church, but also serving beyond the church; it means a life dedicated to God with one purpose: giving him glory through living faithfully in all aspects of our lives. The life that follows God's will requires one to be more than a witness but to be ready to disciple others to live the Godly life that God has commanded us to live. Jesus Christ showed us a perfect example through his death and sacrifice on the cross, demonstrating His obedience to God. Thus, he asked us to be disciples who follow and obey His command. We cannot ignore all seven steps of getting closer to God because each step is important to make us live a completely fulfilled life and prepare ourselves for life afterward. A fulfilled and balanced life comes when we know God and who we are in him. Modern churches continually pursue believers to be all about serving the ministry where they belong and ignore the importance of God's great works through believers in all walks of life. God did not make the church act as the only place to serve. Paul continually commands believers to live out faith in Christ and witness to the Gentiles. He has shown firsthand how God values a life filled with faith and obedience, which ultimately means that God is in our lives and is reaching out to them by using us.

Now, it is time for all of us to represent God truly by testifying the gospel of the grace of God.[375] Everyone needs God in their life. Paul reminds the believers to finish the good race that God has entrusted us to run until the end. We are equipped, but God wants us to go through the journey of training and trusting in him throughout our lives. Thus, we could proclaim that we fought the good fight, finished the race, and kept the faith.[376]

---

[375] Acts 20:24

[376] 2 Timothy 4:7

NOTES

Strong, James LL.D, S.T.D. *The New Strong's Exhaustive Concordance of the Bible.* Nashville, TN: Thomas Nelson Publishers, 1996

Vine, W.E., Unger, Merrill F., White, JR, William *Vine's Complete Expository Dictionary of Old and New Testament Words with Topical Index.* Nashville, TN: Thomas Nelson Publishers, 1996

Holy Bible Containing the Old and New Testaments: The New King James Version, Nashville, TN: Thomas Nelson Publishers, 1996

Additional Resources:

Avery, John *The Name Quest: Explore the Names of God to Grow in Faith and Get to Know Him Better.* New York, NY: Morgan James Publishing, 2015.

Adams, Jay E. *Shepherding God's Flock: A Handbook on Pastoral Ministry, Counseling, and Leadership.* Grand Rapids, MC: Zondervan, 1975.

Banks, Robert. K. *Paul's Idea of Community: The Early House Churches in their Cultural Setting* Peabody, MA: Hendrickson Publishers, 1998.

Beasley-Murray, G. R. *Jesus and the Kingdom of God.* Grand Rapids, MI: Wm. B. Eerdmans Publishing Co., 1986.

Beisner, E. Calvin. *God in Three Persons.* Wheaton, IL: Tyndale House Publishers, Inc., 1984.

Bentley, Chuck., Larry Burkett, *Your Practical Guide for Saving, Spending and Investing.* Knoxville, TN: Crown Financial Ministries, Inc., 2014.

Boettner, Loraine. *The Millennium.* Phillipsburg, NJ: Presbyterian and Reformed Publishing Company, 1991.

Bickersteth, Edward H. *The Trinity.* Grand Rapids, MI: Kregel Publications., 1957.

Bounds, E. M. *The Complete Works of E. M. Bounds.* Radford: Wilder Publications, 2008.

Brott, Richard A. *A Biblical Perspective On Tithing Faithfully: Going From obedience to Blessing.* Jacksonville, FL: ABC Book Publishing, 2008.

Cheung, Vincent *Providence & Revelation.* Boston: Reformation Ministries International, 2003.

Colson, Charles, and Pearcey, Nancy. *How Now Shall We live?.* Wheaton, IL: Tyndale House Publishers, Inc., 1999.

Colson, Charles, and Morse, Anne. *Burden of Truth: Defending Truth in an Age of Unbelief.* Wheaton, IL: Tyndale House Publishers, Inc., 1997.

Cox, William E. *Amillennialism Today.* Phillipsburg, NJ: Presbyterian and Reformed Publishing Co., 1966.

Clouse, Robert G. *The Meaning of the Millennium: Four Views.* Downers Grove, IL: InterVarsity Press, 1977.

Clowney, Edmund. *The Church: Contours of Christian Theology* Downers Grove, IL: Intervarsity Press, 1995.

Corduan, Winfried, *Neighboring Faiths: A Christian Introduction to World Religions.* Downers Grove, IL: IVP Academic, 2012.

Croteau, David A., Bobby Eklund, Ken Hemphill, Reggie Kidd, Gary North, and Scott Preissler, *Perspectives on Tithing: 4 Views.* Nashville, TN: B&H Publishing Group, 2011.

Dayton, Howard *Your Money Counts: now more than ever.* Carol Stream, IL: Tyndale House Publishers, 2011.

Dobson, James. *Love Must Be Tough: The Hope for Families in Crisis.* Waco, TX: Word Books Publisher, 1983.

Dobson, James. *Life on the Edge: A Young Adult's Guide to a Meaningful Future.* Waco, TX: Word Publishing, 1995.

Dockery, David. S. *Biblical Interpretation Then and Now: Contemporary Hermenutics in the Light of the Early Church.* Grand Rapids, MI: Baker Book House, 1992.

Evans, Stephen C. *Despair* Downers Grove, IL: InterVarsity Press, 1964.

Frame, John M. *Medical Ethics: Principles, Persons, and Problems.* Phillipsburg, NJ: Presbyterian and Reformed Publishing Company, 1988.

Frankena, William, and Granrose, John T. *Introductory Readings in Ethics.* Englewood Cliffs, NJ: Prentice-Hall, Inc., 1974.

Ferguson, Sinclair B. *Grow in Grace.* Carlisle, PA: The Banner of Truth Trust, 1989.

Gerstner, John H. *Reasons For Faith.* Grand Rapids, MI: Baker Book House, 1967.

Gish, Duane T. *Evolution: The Challenge of the Fossil Record.* El Cajon, CA: Creation-Life Publishers, 1985.

Gooding, David. *Kingdom: The Letter to the Hebrews for Today* Coleraine, Ireland: Myrtlefield House, 2013.

Gregg, Steve *Revelation: Four Views, A Parallel Commentary.* Dallas, TX: Thomas Nelson, 1997.

Groothuis, Douglas R. *Confronting the New Age: How to Resist a*

Growing Religious Movement. Downers Grove, IL: IVP Academic, 1998.

Harris, Jack. *Freemasonry: The Invisible Cult in Our Midst.* Towson, MD: Jack Harris, 1983.

Hagner, Donald A. *Encountering the Book of Hebrews: An Exposition* Grand Rapids, MI: Baker Academic, 2002.

Helm, Paul. *The Providence of God: Contours of Christian Theology.* Downers Grove, IL: InterVarsity Press, 1994.

Hoekema, Anthony A. *Created in God's Image.* Grand Rapids, MI: Wm. Be. Eerdmans Publishing Company, 1986.

Horton, Michael S. *Putting Amazing Back into Grace: An introduction to Reformed Theology.* Nashville, TN: Thomas Nelson, Inc., 1991.

Hunter, W.Bingham. *The God Who Hears.* Downers Grove, IL: InterVarsity Press, 1986.

Johnson, Philip E. *Defeating Darwinism by Opening Minds.* Downers Grove, IL: InterVarsity Press, 1997.

Klein, William W., and Blomberg, Craigh L., and Hubbard, Robert L. Jr. *Introduction to Biblical Interpretation.* Dallas, TX: Word Publishing, 1993.

Kranz, Jeffrey (Clip Artist). (2014). Free: Bible icons for all 66 books [Clip Art], https://overviewbible.com/free-bible-icons/#download

Little, Paul *How to give away Your Faith.* Madison,IL: InterVarsity Press, 1988.

MacArthur, John F., and Sproul, R. C., and Beeke, Joel., and Gerstner, John., and ArmStrong, John. *Justification By Faith Alone: Affirming the doctrine by which the church and the individuals stands or falls.* Morgan, PA: Soli Deo Gloria Publications, 1995.

Marshall, Howard *New Testament Interpretation: Essays on Principles and Methods.* Grand Rapids, MI: Wm. B. Eerdmans Publishing Company, 1991.

Martin, Walter. *The Maze of Mormonism.* Ventura, CA: Regal Books, 1978.

McCain, Barbara E. *Lessons from Ladies of Faith: Studies in the Lives of Select Women in the Bible That Teach Us Lessons of the Life of Faith for Us Today.* Bloomington, IN: WestBow Press, 2015.

McDermott, Gerald R. *Can Evangelicals Learn From World Religions?: Jesus, Revelation & Religious Traditions.* Downers Grove, IL: IVP Academic, 2000.

McDowell, Josh, and Stewart, Don. *Answers to Tough Questions skeptics ask about the Christian faith.* San Bernardino, CA: Here's Life Publishers, Inc., 1980.

Miethe, Terry L., Habermas, Gary R. *Why believe? God Exists!: Rethinking the Case For God and Christianity.* Joplin, MO: College Press Publishing Company., 1993.

Moreland, J.P. *Love Your God with All Your Mind: The Role of Reason in the Life of the Soul.* Colorado Spring, CO: NavPress Publishing Group, 1997.

Morris, Gregory K. *In Pursuit of Leadership: Principles and Practices from the Life of Moses* LakeLand, FL: Leadership Press, 2013.

Pearcey, Nancy R., and Thaxton, Charles B. *The Soul of Science: Christian Faith and Natural Philosophy*, Wheaton, IL: Crossway Books, 1994.

Pink, A.W. *An Exposition of Hebrews* West Linn, OR: Monergism Books, 2018.

Pinnock, Clark., Rice, Richard., Sanders, John., Hasker, William., and Basinger, David. The Openness of God: A Biblical Challenge to the Traditional Understanding of God. Downers Grove, IL: Intervarsity Press., 1994.

Piper, John, and Grudem, Wayne. *Recovering Biblical Manhood and Womanhood: A Response to Evangelical Feminism.* Wheaton, IL: Crossway Books, 1991.

Poythress, Vern S. *God Centered Biblical Interpretation.* Phillipsburg, NJ: P&R Publishing, 1999.

Poythress, Vern S. *The Shadow of Christ in the Law of Moses.* Brentwood, TN: Wolgemuth & Hyatt, Publishers, Inc., 1999.

Quiggle, James D. *Why Christians Should Not Tithe: A History of Tithing and A Biblical Paradigm for Christian Giving.* Eugene, OR: Wipf and Stock Publshers, 2009.

Qureshi, Nabeel. *No One but One: Allah or Jesus?* Grand Rapids, MI: Zondervan, 2016.

Rae, Scott B., and Wong, Kenman L., *Beyond Integrity: A Judeo-Christian Approach to Business Ethics.* Grand Rapids, MI: Zondervan Academic, 2012.

Ramsey, Dave. *The Total Money Makeover: A Proven Plan for Financial Fitness.* Nashville, TN: Thomas Nelson, 2009.

Reisinger, Ernest C. *Lord and Christ: The Implications of Lordship for Faith and Life.* Phillipsburg, NJ: P&R Publishing., 1994.

Reisinger, Ernest C. *Today's Evangelism: Its Message and Methods.* Phillipsburg, NJ: Craig Press., 1982.

Rhodes, Ron *Basic Bible Prophecy: Essential Facts Every Christian Should Know* Eugene, OR: Harvest House Publishers, 2021.

Richardson, Ronald W. *Couples in Conflict: A Family Systems Approach to Marriage Counseling.* Minneapolis, MN: Fortress Press, 2010.

Ryrie, Charles C. *Dispensationalism Today.* Chicago, IL: Moody Press, 1974.

Saucy, Robert L. *The Church in God's Program.* Chicago, IL: Moody Press, 1972.

Sanders, J. Oswald. K. *Spiritual Leadership: Principles of Excellence for Every Believer* Chicago, IL: Moody Publishers, 2007.

Silva, Mooises. *Exploration in Exegetical Method: Galatians As A Test Case.* Grand Rapids, MI: Baker Books, 1996.

Stein, Robert H. *Jesus the Messiah: A Survey of the Life of Christ.* Downers Grove, IL: InterVarsity Press, 1996.

Sproul, R. C. *Faith Alone: The Evangelical Doctrine of Justification.* Grand Rapids, MI: Baker Books, 1995.

Stott, John. *Evangelical Truth: A personal Plea for Unity, Integrity and Faithfulness.* Cumbria, England: Langham Global Library, 1995

Tripp, Paul David. *Lead: 12 Gospel Principles for Leadership in the Church* Wheaton, IL: Crossway, 2020.

Trucksess, Kurt. *Hebrews: Fix Your Eyes on Jesus* Spirit Lake, IA: Christ2rCulture, 2008.

Wilson, Marvin R. *Our Father Abraham: Jewish Roots of the Christian Faith.* Grand Rapids, MI: Wm. B. Eerdmans Publishing Company, 2014.

Wright, Christopher J.H. *Old Testament Ethics for The People Of God.* Downers Grove, IL: InterVarsity Press, 2004.

Wright, N.T. *Hebrews for Everyone* Louisville, KY: Westminster John Knox Press, 2004.

ABOUT THE AUTHOR

Jonathan "Dj" Kim serves at Skyline Grace Church as senior pastor. He received his doctorate in ministry from Colorado Theological Seminary. He lives with his wife, Nancy, his son, Joshua, and his daughter, Johanna, in Garden Grove, CA.

www.ingramcontent.com/pod-product-compliance
Lightning Source LLC
Chambersburg PA
CBHW061328040426
42444CB00011B/2813